THE
GARDEN
PLANNER

THE
GARDEN
PLANNER

Innovative designs for small spaces

PETER McHOY

LORENZ BOOKS

This edition is published by Lorenz Books

Lorenz Books is an imprint of Anness Publishing Ltd
Hermes House, 88–89 Blackfriars Road, London SE1 8HA
tel. 020 7401 2077; fax 020 7633 9499
www.lorenzbooks.com; info@anness.com

© Anness Publishing Ltd 1998, 2003

This edition distributed in the UK by Aurum Press Ltd, 25 Bedford Avenue, London WC1B 3AT;
tel. 020 7637 3225; fax 020 7580 2469

This edition distributed in the USA and Canada by National Book Network, 4720 Boston Way, Lanham,
MD 20706; tel. 301 459 3366; fax 301 459 1705; www.nbnbooks.com

This edition distributed in Australia by Pan Macmillan Australia, Level 18, St Martins Tower, 31 Market St,
Sydney, NSW 2000; tel. 1300 135 113; fax 1300 135 103; customer.service@macmillan.com.au

This edition distributed in New Zealand by David Bateman Ltd, 30 Tarndale Grove, Off Bush Road, Albany,
Auckland; tel. (09) 415 7664; fax (09) 415 8892

A CIP catalogue record for this book is available from the British Library.

Publisher Joanna Lorenz
Senior Editor Catherine Barry
Designer Michael Morey
Illustrator Neil Bulpitt

Previously published as *The Ultimate Garden Planner*

3 5 7 9 10 8 6 4 2

In the directory section of this book, each plant is given a hardiness rating. The temperature ranges are as follows: frost tender – may be damaged by
temperatures below 5°C (41°F); half hardy – can withstand temperatures down to 0°C (32°F); frost hardy – can withstand temperatures down to -5°C
(23°F); fully hardy – can withstand temperatures down to -15°C (5°F).
In the United States, throughout the Sun Belt states, from Florida, across the Gulf Coast, south Texas, southern deserts to Southern California and
coastal regions, annuals are planted in the autumn, bloom in the winter and spring, and die at the beginning of summer.

■ ABOVE
Odd corners of the garden can become a focal point with
a feature such as a birdbath.

■ PAGES ONE, TWO AND THREE
Even gardens where plants dominate benefit from a few
structural plants.

Wild areas of the garden can be wonderful too.
Sloping gardens can be an asset not a drawback.

CONTENTS

....

■ ABOVE
Be prepared to be bold with a town garden, and make the most
of structural elements.

INTRODUCTION

....

Few of us are totally content with our gardens. Despite the immense pleasure we derive from them, there's always something that could be better. Most of us long for a larger garden, a few for something smaller and more manageable, but the vast majority of us have to make the best of our existing plot. Improving it, coaxing the maximum impact from it, is an enjoyable challenge that most of us would rise to – if only we knew how.

Gardening is about growing plants, but the setting in which we place them is probably the element that makes a garden appealing or otherwise. Tastes in gardening styles vary as much as in other aspects of living, and what appeals to one person may not appeal to another, but the test of a good garden design is whether it appeals to *you*. This book sets out to help you create a garden that reflects your taste, your personality.

It also lifts the lid on the magic box of imagination and inspiration. It shows you what other enthusiastic gardeners have done, and how others have made the most of sometimes unpromising plots. This is an eminently practical book, too, and it will guide you through drawing your first plans to planting and simple garden construction.

■ ABOVE
A garden that looks lived in will be used.

■ OPPOSITE
Paths and walls form a backdrop for plants.

GARDEN PLANNING MADE EASY

You can have your garden designed and constructed by professionals, but it will cost a great deal of money, and the chances are that it won't give you as much satisfaction as having created a garden by your own efforts.

This chapter explains the basic techniques for simple garden design, but it's up to you as to how you interpret them and what you create with the tools provided. The remaining chapters are packed with inspirational ideas, but only you can decide what's right for your garden. Tastes in gardens vary as much as in interior decor and preferences in music or art. The acid test of whether your new design has worked is whether it pleases you.

Use the techniques suggested to experiment on paper – you will soon develop skills that will enable you to design your garden with confidence.

■ ABOVE
A striking garden, which uses water and paving in a highly structured design.

■ OPPOSITE
An informal, country-style garden, with colourful borders overflowing with
flowers and shrubs, yet with a clear sense of design.

TAKING STOCK

If you're planning and planting a new garden from a virgin plot of land, then your starting point is a wish list of features to incorporate.

But if you are redesigning an existing garden, it's also important to decide whether there are features that you would like to retain.

Never let an existing feature dictate your new garden, unless you have no alternative but to work around it. For instance, you may be limited by what you can do with a large tree or unsightly garage. While you may not want the disruption of digging up the drive and moving the garage, don't be dictated to by the presence of ordinary garden paths. They may be tiring to lift, but a straight path down the centre of a narrow garden will limit your ability to be creative with your new design.

Make lists of what has to stay and what you want to work around and improve.

THE WISH LIST

Make your wish list before you attempt your design. It is unlikely to be fulfilled completely, but setting down those things that are a priority to you should ensure that the most important features are included.

Everyone has different preferences, so decide which features you regard as essential (it may be something as mundane as a clothes drier or as stimulating as a water feature), those that are important but less essential for your ideal garden, and those elements that you regard simply as desirable.

While designing your garden, keep in mind those features listed as essential. Try to incorporate as many of them as possible, but

don't cram in so many that a strong sense of design is sacrificed.

It will immediately become apparent if the list of the most desirable features is not feasible within the limited space available,

but you will probably be able to introduce some of the more important ones. However, attempt to include only those features ticked (checked) simply as desirable if you have space.

GARDEN PRIORITIES

	Essential	Important	Desirable
Flowerbeds	[ ]	[ ]	[ ]
Herbaceous border	[ ]	[ ]	[ ]
Shrub border	[ ]	[ ]	[ ]
Trees	[ ]	[ ]	[ ]
Lawn	[ ]	[ ]	[ ]
Gravelled area	[ ]	[ ]	[ ]
Paved area/patio	[ ]	[ ]	[ ]
Built-in barbecue	[ ]	[ ]	[ ]
Garden seats/furniture	[ ]	[ ]	[ ]
Rock garden	[ ]	[ ]	[ ]
Pond	[ ]	[ ]	[ ]
Other water feature	[ ]	[ ]	[ ]
Wildlife area	[ ]	[ ]	[ ]
Greenhouse/conservatory	[ ]	[ ]	[ ]
Summerhouse	[ ]	[ ]	[ ]
Tool shed	[ ]	[ ]	[ ]
Fruit garden	[ ]	[ ]	[ ]
Herb garden	[ ]	[ ]	[ ]
Vegetable garden	[ ]	[ ]	[ ]
Trellis/pergola/arch	[ ]	[ ]	[ ]
Sandpit/play area	[ ]	[ ]	[ ]
Clothes drier/line	[ ]	[ ]	[ ]
Dustbin (trash can)	[ ]	[ ]	[ ]
Compost heap	[ ]	[ ]	[ ]
. . . .	[ ]	[ ]	[ ]
. . . .	[ ]	[ ]	[ ]
. . . .	[ ]	[ ]	[ ]
. . . .	[ ]	[ ]	[ ]
. . . .	[ ]	[ ]	[ ]
. . . .	[ ]	[ ]	[ ]
. . . .	[ ]	[ ]	[ ]
. . . .	[ ]	[ ]	[ ]

■ OPPOSITE
The initial sketch can be simple and need contain only the basic dimensions. Do not bother with anything that you do not intend to include in the new garden.

SURVEYING AND MEASURING

It is much better – and less expensive – to make your mistakes on paper first, rather than in the garden itself. Start by making a sketch of the garden as it is, and then work up your ideas.

If your garden is large, divide it into sections that can be pieced together later, but for a small garden the whole area will go on to a single sheet of paper. Leave space around the edge for measurements.

Write down the measurements of all the main features such as a tree, path or garage. Do not include anything that you are already sure you will not retain. Small rectangular gardens are very easy to measure. Sometimes the boundary can be calculated simply by counting fence panels and multiplying up the length of a fence panel and post. Most other features can be fixed by measuring at right angles from the boundary.

If the shape of the garden is more complicated, it is usually possible to determine a position by laying a piece of string at right angles from the known straight edge, then measuring at right angles from this line.

WHAT YOU WILL NEED

■ A 30m (100ft) tape measure – preferably plasticized fabric as this is easy to work with but does not stretch.

■ A 1.8m (6ft) steel rule for short measurements.

■ Pegs to mark out positions, and to hold one end of the tape in position (meat skewers can be used to hold the end of the tape).

■ Pencils, sharpener and eraser.

■ Clipboard with graph paper.

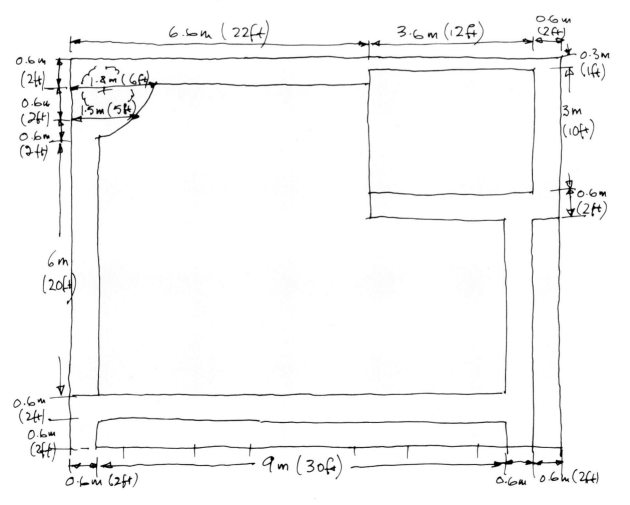

PUTTING THE PLAN ON PAPER

The exciting part of redesigning a garden comes when the basic structure is on the drawing board and you can start to work magical transformations as you try to test your ideas. Drawing to scale is the next step to reach this goal.

With the rough sketch from the garden drawn accurately to scale, the stimulating part of garden planning can begin. It is when dreams can start to be translated into reality. Making an accurate scale drawing of your existing garden is an essential starting point if you want to simplify the design work that follows.

The rough sketch must be transferred to a scale drawing before any detailed plans can be sketched out. Drawing it to scale will help you to calculate the amount of any paving required, and also enable you to tailor beds, borders and lawns to sizes that will involve the least amount of cutting of hard materials such as paving slabs or bricks.

Use graph paper for your scale drawing. Pads are adequate for a small garden or a section of a larger one, but if your garden is big, buy a large sheet (available from art and stationers' shops).

Use a scale that enables you to fit the plan on to your sheet of graph paper (or several taped together). For most small gardens, a scale of 1:50 (2cm to 1m or ¼in to 1ft) is about right; for a large garden, however, 1:100 (1cm to 1m or ⅛in to 1ft) might be better.

Draw the basic outline of the garden and the position of the house first, including the position of any doors and windows if relevant. Then add all the major features that you are likely to retain. You should have all the necessary measurements on the freehand sketch that you made in the garden.

Omit any features that you are sure will be eliminated from the new design, to keep it as uncluttered as possible. In this example, the summerhouse has been drawn in because it was considered to be in a good position and would be difficult to move. Although the corner tree was removed in the final design, it was included at this stage as a different design might have made use of it.

QUICK ON THE DRAW

Try these tips if you are not used to drawing garden plans:

■ Draw the outline of the garden first, together with the position of the house and any other major features, and make sure you have the correct measurements for these before filling in any of the other elements.

■ Next, draw in those elements that are easy to position, such as rectangular flowerbeds, a circular pond or the garden shed, if you are reasonably certain of their position and know they will remain in your new design.

■ Ink in those elements of the garden that are fixed and will not change, such as boundaries and paths that you know you will not move. Draw the more movable garden features in pencil first, as it is quite likely that you may have to make slight adjustments before the plan is complete. Ink them in when you know everything is in its correct place.

■ Use a pair of compasses to draw curves and circles if possible. Not all curves are suitable for this treatment, but you can buy flexible rules that can be bent into any reasonable curve.

USING YOUR PLAN

1 Even expert designers make a number of rough sketches of possible designs before finalizing the chosen one, so devise a way of using your master outline again and again without having to keep redrawing it. One way is to make a number of photocopies or use tracing paper.

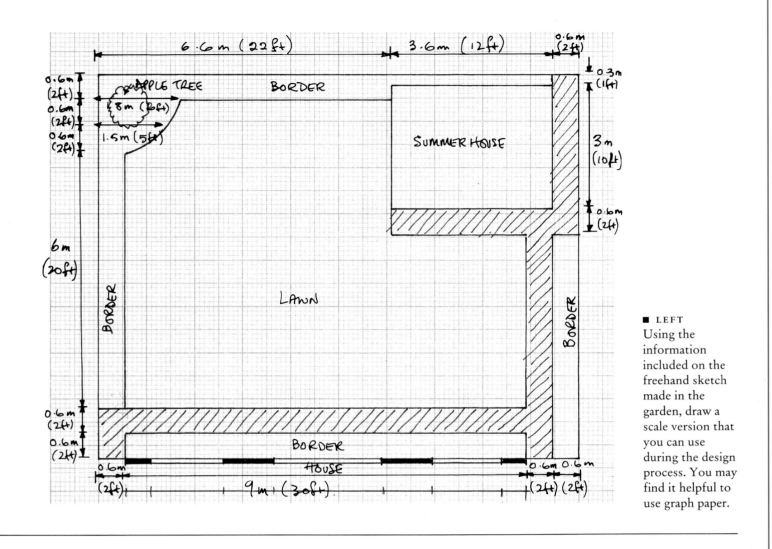

6·6 m (22 ft) 3·6 m (12 ft) 0·6 m (2ft)

0·6 m (2ft)
0·6 m (2ft)
0·6 m (2ft)

APPLE TREE BORDER

8 m (26ft)

1·5 m (5ft)

0·3 m (1ft)

SUMMER HOUSE

3 m (10ft)

0·6 m (2ft)

6 m (20ft)

LAWN

BORDER

BORDER

0·6 m (2ft)
0·6 m (2ft)

BORDER

HOUSE

0·6 m (2ft) 9 m (30ft) 0·6 m 0·6 m (2ft) (2ft)

■ LEFT
Using the information included on the freehand sketch made in the garden, draw a scale version that you can use during the design process. You may find it helpful to use graph paper.

2 If you have a drawing board, simply use tracing paper overlays for your roughs while experimenting with ideas. If you do not have a drawing board and your garden is small, you may be able to use a clipboard to hold the tracing paper firmly in position.

3 Film and pens of the type used for overhead projection sheets are effective if you prefer to use colours that can easily be wiped off for correction.

4 Try drawing and cutting out scale features that you want to include in your finished design, such as a raised pond, patio furniture or raised beds. These can be moved around until they look right, but they should be used as aids only once the overall design has been formulated in your mind. If you try to design your garden around the few key symbols that you have placed, it will almost certainly lack coherence.

CREATING YOUR DESIGN

The difficult part of redesigning or improving your garden is making a start. Once you start drawing, the ideas are sure to flow, especially if you have other gardens in mind that you like and can use as inspiration and a starting point. Don't attempt to copy someone else's plan in detail – it probably won't fit the size or style of your property, or your requirements – but such plans are excellent to refer to for inspiration when developing your own design.

If you decide on a garden with strong lines, rather than irregular flowering borders, it is worth deciding on whether you are going to plan a rectangular or diagonal or circular design. Any of these can be adapted to suit the size of your garden, and in the case of the circular pattern you might want to include overlapping circles. Where circles join, try to make any transitional curves gradual rather than abrupt. Whichever you choose, draw a grid on top of your plan to aid design (see opposite page). In a small garden surrounded by fencing, it can be useful to base the rectangular and diagonal grids on the spacing of fence posts – usually about 1.8m (6ft) apart.

A rectangular grid has been used in the example opposite, but as part of the trial-and-error phase it is worth trying different grids. A diagonal grid is often effective where the house is set in a large garden with plenty of space at the sides. The patio can be positioned at a 45-degree angle at the corner of the house, for example.

The size and shape of the garden will usually dictate the best grid, but if in doubt, try the other possibilities to see which one is most appropriate.

Bear in mind that many excellent, prize-winning gardens are created without such a grid, and sometimes these have, to some extent, evolved in a more flowing manner, developing feature by feature. Grids may help you, but do not hesitate to adopt a more freestyle approach if this comes more naturally.

LOOKING FOR INSPIRATION

Don't despair if inspiration does not come easily, or initial attempts seem disappointing. If you try these tips, you will almost certainly produce workable plans that you will be pleased with:

■ Look through books and magazines to decide which style of garden you like: formal or informal; the emphasis on plants or on hard landscaping; mainly foliage, texture and ground cover or lots of colourful flowers; straight edges or curved and flowing lines.

■ With the style decided, look at as many garden pictures as possible and for design ideas that appeal. Do not be influenced by individual plants; these can be changed.

■ Choose a grid, if applicable, and draw this on to your plan. This will help you think ideas through on logical lines.

■ Start sketching lots of designs but do not attempt to perfect them at this stage. Just explore ideas.

■ Do not concern yourself with planning planting schemes at this stage – concentrate on patterns and lines.

■ Do not spend time drawing in paving patterns or choosing materials yet.

■ Make a short list of those overall outlines that you like best. Then forget them for a day. It pays to take a fresh look at things after a short break.

■ If you still like one of your original roughs, begin work on that, filling in details like paving, surface textures such as gravel, and the position of focal point plants, etc. Don't include any planting plans at this stage.

■ If your original roughs lack appeal when you look at them again, repeat the process with another batch of ideas. You will probably see ways of improving some of your earlier efforts, so things will be easier this time around.

■ If you find it difficult to visualize sizes, peg the design out at full size on the ground with string, then modify the layout and your plan if necessary.

BEGIN THE DESIGN

1 Draw in any existing features to be retained (in this example the summerhouse), and the chosen grid (unless you want an informal style where a grid may be inappropriate). Use a different colour for the grid lines, to prevent the plan becoming cluttered and confused.

2 Use overlays (or photocopies) to experiment with a range of designs. Even if the first attempt looks satisfactory, try a number of variations. You can always come back to your first idea if it turns out to be the best one.

At this stage, do not include details such as patio furniture or individual plants (except for key focal-point plants and important trees or shrubs). When you have a design that you like, pencil in things like patio furniture (or use scale cut-out features if you prefer).

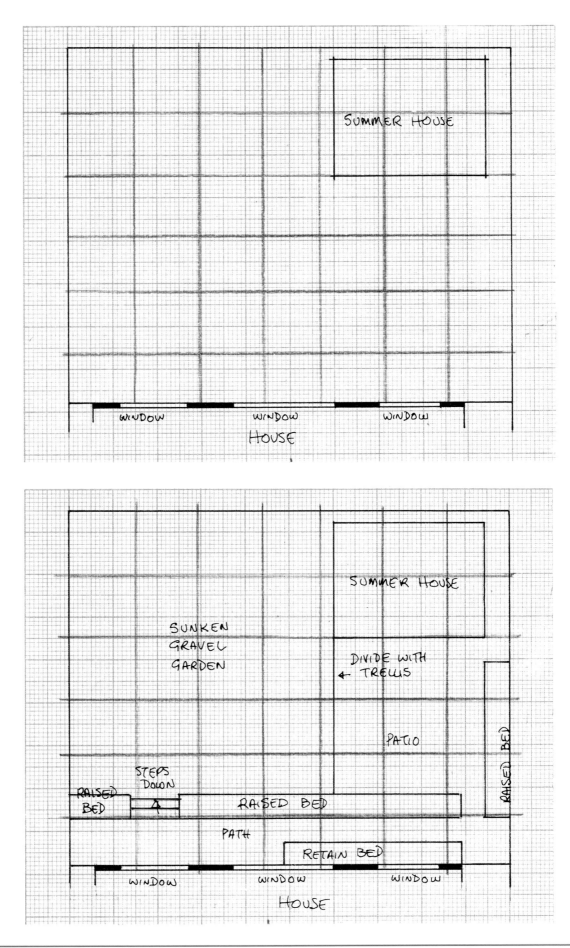

BASIC PATTERNS

Having decided on the style of garden that you want, and the features that you need to incorporate, it's time to tackle the much more difficult task of applying the theory to your own garden.

STARTING POINTS
The chances are that your garden will be the wrong size or shape, or the situation or outlook inappropriate to the style of garden that you have admired. The way around this impasse is to keep in mind a style without attempting to recreate it closely.

If you can't visualize the whole of your back or front garden as, say, a stone or Japanese garden, it may be possible to include the feature as an element within a more general design.

If you analyse successful formal garden designs, most fall into one of the three basic patterns described here, though clever planting and variations on the themes almost always result in individual designs.

■ **RIGHT**
CIRCULAR THEMES These are effective at disguising the predictable shape of a rectangular garden. Circular lawns, patios and beds are all options, and you only need to overlap and interlock a few circles to create a stylish garden. Plants fill the gaps between curved areas and straight edges.

Using a pair of compasses, try various combinations of circles to see whether you can create an attractive pattern. Be prepared to vary the radii and to overlap the circles if necessary.

■ **OPPOSITE LEFT**
DIAGONAL THEMES This device creates a sense of space by taking the eye along and across the garden. Start by drawing grid lines at 45 degrees to the house or main fence. Then draw in the design, using the grid as a guide.

■ **OPPOSITE RIGHT**
RECTANGULAR THEMES This is a popular choice, and many garden plans end up with a rectangular theme – even though there may have been no conscious effort to do so. The device is effective if you want to create a formal look, or wish to divide up a long, narrow garden into smaller sections.

FORMAL AND INFORMAL

If you like straight lines and everything neat and clearly done to a plan, a formal garden should please, but for some gardeners an informal, more casual style that looks more like a simple setting for plants is likely to have more appeal. Informal gardens are also more adaptable to family use, with the lawn providing opportunities for play as well as relaxation for adults.

It's important to decide at an early stage whether the formal designs represented by some of the grids described earlier are right for your style of gardening, or even whether they fit your lifestyle – a growing family may prefer a more casual style of garden. Those who are interested in flowers and foliage rather than hard landscaping are more likely to feel at home among sweeping borders, hidden paths, and seats tucked into arbours or overlooking a wildlife pond.

Anyone who loves the informality of cottage gardens, which may be little more than a couple of borders either side of a path or lawn, may find a very structured garden unappealing. With informal gardens, it is the positioning of plants that gives it gardener appeal. Even the style of planting may be less planned, with self-sown seedlings coming up between other plants in the border, or among the paving.

If this is your kind of garden, follow your instinct, but remember that focal points and flowing curves are still important. Arbours, pergolas and ornaments, well-positioned garden seats, and a sense of overall planning and good planting sense are just as relevant in this kind of garden as in a more structured one.

■ RIGHT AND OPPOSITE
These two designs show how different a garden of the same size can look depending on whether a formal or informal style is used. Deciding on the degree of formality in the design comes early in the planning stage.

KEY TO PLAN

1 Ornament (on plinth)
2 Herb garden
3 Shed
4 Trellis
5 Climbers (e.g. ivy, parthenocissus and clematis) against trellis
6 Sundial or birdbath
7 Mixed border
8 Large pot with shrubs/shaped clipped box
9 Garden bench
10 Pool with fountain
11 Arch
12 Group of large shrubs
13 Screen-block wall
14 Patio furniture
15 Vegetable garden
16 Trellis arch
17 Path
18 House

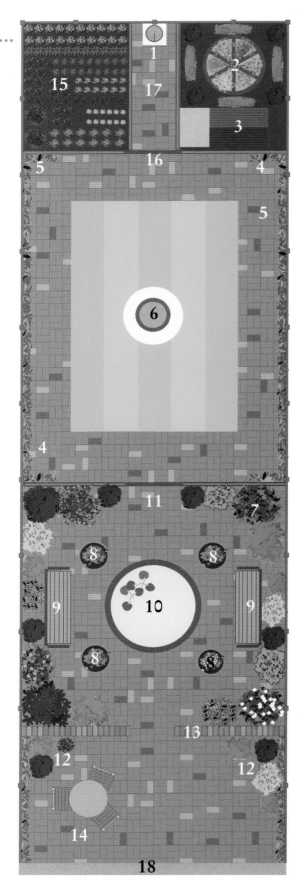

INFORMALITY

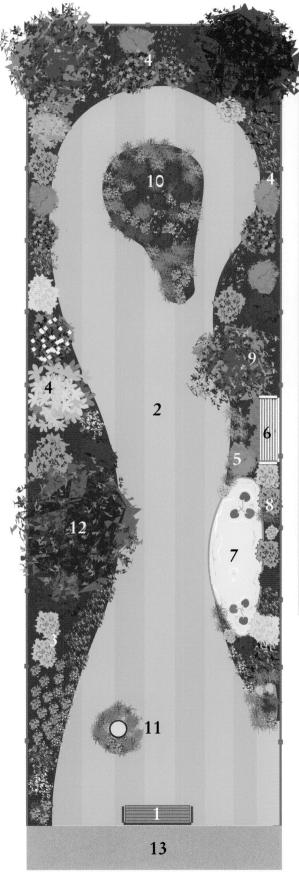

■ BELOW
The planting here gives the impression of informality, but the symmetry of the design is formal.

KEY TO PLAN

1 Garden bench
2 Lawn
3 Herbaceous plants and bulbs
4 Shrubs
5 Thymes and other aromatic herbs planted between crazy paving
6 White metal garden bench
7 Pond
8 Bog garden
9 Red-stemmed dogwood
10 Dwarf conifers and heathers
11 Birdbath or sundial, with plants around base
12 Tree
13 House

UNUSUAL SHAPES

It may be possible to turn a problem shape to your advantage by using its unusual outline to create a garden that stands out from others in the street. Because of its originality, what was once a difficult area to plant will soon become the object of other gardeners' envy. The seven designs shown here illustrate how difficult sites can, with imagination and some careful planning, produce promising gardens.

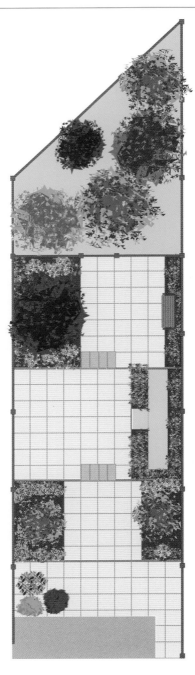

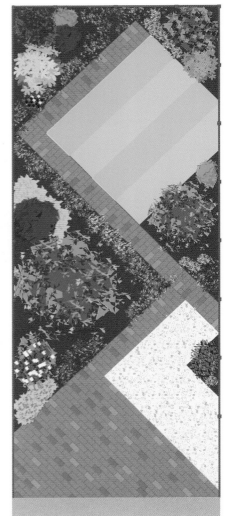

■ **ABOVE LEFT AND ABOVE CENTRE**
LONG AND NARROW The plan on the left shows a design based on a circular theme. The paved area near the house can be used as a patio, and the one at the far end for drying the washing, largely out of sight from the house. Alternatively, if the end of the garden receives more sun, reverse the roles of the paved areas. Taking the connecting path across the garden at an angle, and using small trees or large shrubs to prevent the eye travelling straight along the sides, creates the impression of a garden to be explored. The plan on the right shows the use of diagonals to achieve a similar effect.

■ **ABOVE**
LONG AND TAPERING If the garden is long and pointed, try screening off the main area, leaving a gateway or arch to create the impression of more garden beyond while not revealing the actual shape. The tapering end of the garden could be used as an orchard, as here, or a vegetable garden.

Staggering the three paved areas, with small changes of level, adds interest and prevents the garden looking too long. At the same time, a long view has been retained to give the impression of size.

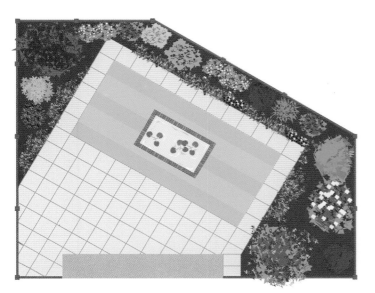

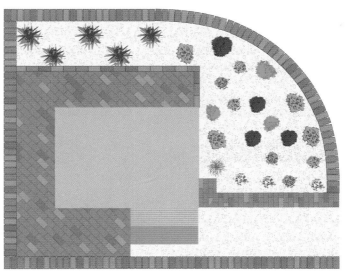

■ ABOVE

ANGULAR CORNER SITE Corner sites are often larger than other plots in the same road, and offer scope for some interesting designs. This one has been planned to make the most of the extra space at the side of the house, which has become the main feature of the garden instead of the more usual back or front areas.

■ ABOVE

CURVED CORNER SITE Curved corner gardens are more difficult to design effectively. In this plan the house is surrounded by a patio on the left-hand side, and a low wall partitions the patio from the rest of the garden, making it more private. For additional interest, a path separates the drive from the gravel garden. Gravel and boulders, punctuated by striking plants such as phormiums and yuccas, effectively marry the straight edges with the bold curve created by the corner site.

■ RIGHT

L-SHAPED L-shaped gardens offer plenty of scope. Even in a small garden, the opportunity to walk around and explore an area that cannot be seen from one place is a considerable plus point. This plan shows the clever use of focal points – a tree seat and a seat at the far end – to create a reason for exploring the garden. The patio area, which is partially covered by overhead beams, is separated from the rest of the garden by raised flowerbeds.

■ ABOVE

SQUARE AND SQUAT A small square site like this offers little scope for elaborate design, so keep to a few simple elements. To give the impression of greater space the viewpoint has been angled diagonally across the garden. For additional interest, the timber decking is slightly raised, creating a change of level. A small lawn can be difficult to cut in a tiny garden, but you could try an alternative to grass, such as chamomile, which needs trimming only infrequently.

The diagonal theme helps to counter the basic rectangular shape of the garden and makes the most of available space.

COPING WITH SLOPES

Sloping sites are particularly difficult to plan on paper, and they are much more challenging to design in general than flat sites. As sloping gardens vary so much in the degree of slope – whether the garden slopes down from the house or upwards – as well as size and aspect, it is also more difficult to adapt designs created by others. Although sloping gardens are difficult to design, the drawbacks can be turned into advantages. Changes of level can add interest and provide an excellent setting for rock gardens and cascading "streams".

KEY TO PLAN

1 Patio
2 Wall fountain with small pool
3 Bricks or clay pavers
4 Rock garden bank sloping downhill and towards a flat paved area
5 "Stream" with cascades
6 Pond, disappearing behind shrubs
7 Small retaining wall
8 Shed for tools and mower

9 Shrubs
10 Summerhouse with views across garden and attractive view below garden
11 Lawn
12 Gravel with alpines
13 Gravel area with natural paving
14 Pavers mixed with paving slabs
15 Trees and shrubs
16 Ornament (on plinth)
17 House

■ **ABOVE RIGHT**
SLOPING DOWN A downward-sloping garden with an attractive view is much easier to design successfully than an upward-sloping one. If the outlook is unattractive, however, it may be advisable to screen the lowest part of the garden with shrubs and small trees and use it as the main sitting area.

This plan demonstrates several important principles when designing a sloping garden, and unusually combines terraces with a natural slope. Terracing is expensive and time-consuming: it involves earth-moving, and retaining

walls on strong foundations have to be built. Moving the topsoil from one area to lower down the slope is unsatisfactory as part of the garden will be left with subsoil at the surface for planting – a recipe for disappointment. Topsoil should be set aside, the ground levelled, and then the topsoil returned, which is labour-intensive.

Terracing provides flat areas on which to walk and relax, and this design includes flat areas along the length of the garden. As these have been used for hard surfaces, the problem of subsoil and topsoil does not arise. Retaining the

natural slope for a large part of the garden reduces the amount of structural work required and cost.

Although there are some retaining walls, the two walls that zigzag down the garden are stepped so that they remain just above the surrounding ground.

Retaining a large area of naturally sloping ground also provides an ideal setting for rock outcrops and an artificial stream with a series of cascades.

Taking a path across the garden at an angle makes it seem less steep. A path that runs in a straight line down the slope only serves to emphasize the drop.

■ LEFT

■ LEFT

If the slope falls away from the house suddenly, building a raised patio like this will provide a level area and avoid the use of steps immediately outside the door.

■ RIGHT

SLOPING UPWARDS An upward slope is a challenge. Distant views are not a possibility, and even upper floors may look out on to a bank. Terracing in this situation can look oppressive, but a "secret" garden full of meandering paths flanked by shrubs is an effective way of dealing with the slope. Some retaining walls are usually necessary, but if planted with shrubs, the effect will be masked and the plants on the lower terraces will hide the upper walls and banks.

Lawns are difficult to accommodate on a steeply sloping site, and difficult to mow too, as mowers are awkward to carry up steps and steep ramps for access. It is generally best to avoid grass lawns, but use a grass "alternative" in a small levelled area. Chamomile and thyme require only an occasional trim with shears, which for a small area is not an onerous job.

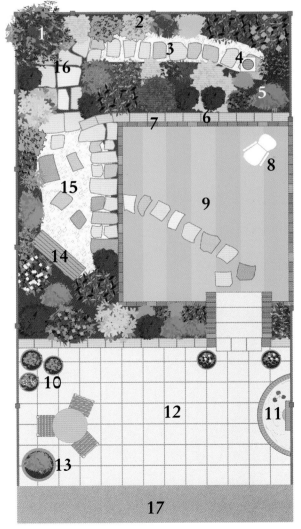

KEY TO PLAN

1 Small tree
2 Shrubs
3 Natural stone paving slabs set in gravel
4 Ornament on plinth as a focal point
5 Dwarf shrubs on bank
6 Retaining wall
7 Brick edge
8 Lounger or deckchair
9 Thyme or chamomile lawn
10 Plants in containers
11 Wall fountain with small pool beneath
12 Patio
13 Shrub or small tree in large tub
14 Seat
15 Natural stone paving set in gravel
16 Natural stone path
17 House

FRONT GARDENS

Front gardens have special problems – especially if they have to accommodate a drive for the car. Perhaps for that reason they frequently lack interest and look uninspiring, yet it's the front garden that visitors see first, so it's worth making a special effort to create a good impression. Even enthusiastic gardeners with delightful back gardens are often let down by a dull front garden. Here two small front gardens with typical problems have been transformed by a little creative thinking and careful planning.

COUNTRY COTTAGE LOOK
Gardens don't come much more uninspired than this: a concrete drive, a small narrow flowerbed on the paved patio in front of the window, a narrow border along the edge of the garden, and a single flowering cherry tree placed in the centre of a rectangular lawn. However, the solution for this garden was a simple one, as the redesigned garden on the right shows. The cottage-garden style includes plants of all kinds which grow and mingle happily together with minimum intervention.

Besides being a short cut to the front door, the stepping stones encourage exploration of the garden and its plants. You actually walk through the planting, which cascades and tumbles around the paving slabs. The garden design has been reversed, with plants forming the heart of the garden rather than being peripherals around the edge. Don't be afraid to dig up a lawn – you can retain the year-round colour by planting evergreen shrubs and seasonal flowers.

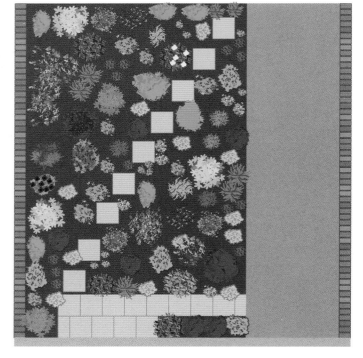

PROBLEMS
▌ Although the cherry is spectacular in flower, and provides a show of autumn colour, it is attractive for only a few weeks of the year. Its present position precludes any major redesign, so it is best removed.
▌ Unclothed wooden fences contribute to the drab appearance.
▌ Small flowerbeds like these lack impact, and are too small for the imaginative use of shrubs or herbaceous perennials.

SOLUTIONS
▌ The lawn and tree have been removed, and the whole area planted with a mixture of dwarf shrubs, herbaceous perennials, hardy annuals, and lots of bulbs for spring interest.
▌ Stepping stones have been provided for those who want to take a short cut (they also make access for weeding easier).
▌ The fences have been replaced by low walls to make the garden appear less confined.

IMPACT WITH PRIVACY

Being on a corner, this garden is a jumble of shapes and angles, and as originally constructed lacks any sense of design. With its new look, the old curved path has been retained because its thick concrete base and the drain inspection cover within it would have made it difficult to move, but all the other lines have been simplified and more appropriate plants used. The curved, flowing stream along the right-hand side adds movement and sound to the garden.

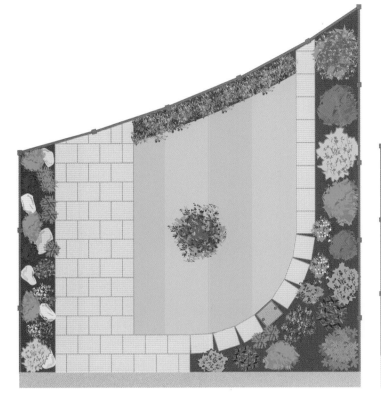

PROBLEMS

▌ The bed along the left-hand side was a rock garden, but rock gardens are seldom successful on a flat site in a small garden.

▌ The tree would have grown large, eventually casting considerable shade and dominating the garden.

▌ Small beds like this, used for seasonal bedding, are colourful in summer but can lack interest in winter. This curve sits uneasily with the straight edge at one end and the curve of the path at the other.

SOLUTIONS

▌ The rock garden has been paved so that the cultivated area is not divided by the drive.

▌ Gravel replaces the lawn. This requires minimal maintenance and acts as a good foil for the plants.

▌ Dwarf and medium-sized conifers create height and cover, and therefore a degree of privacy. Using species and varieties in many shades of green and gold, and choosing a range of shapes, makes this part of the garden interesting throughout the year.

▌ Stepping stones add further interest. Because it isn't possible to see where the stepping stones lead to from either end (the conifers hide the route), a sense of mystery is added which tempts the visitor to explore.

▌ The existing path has been retained but covered with slate crazy paving to make it more interesting.

▌ A pond creates a water feature and also attracts wildlife.

▌ The awkward, narrow curving strip has been turned into a stream with circulating water flowing over a cascade into the pond at one end.

▌ LEFT
Instead of a lawn with a few flowerbeds around the edge, this small front garden has been planted in cottage-garden style. It is packed with interest throughout the year.

CREATING ILLUSIONS

Sometimes it's good to deceive – at least deceive the eye into thinking your garden is bigger or better than it really is! Try some of these simple devices to solve some of those difficult problems. The few simple forms of visual deception described here should enable you to make your garden look larger than it really is, helping to distract the eye from unattractive features by making the most of the positive.

■ **RIGHT**
First impressions here are of a large garden extending beyond the arch, yet it's an illusion done with a mirror!

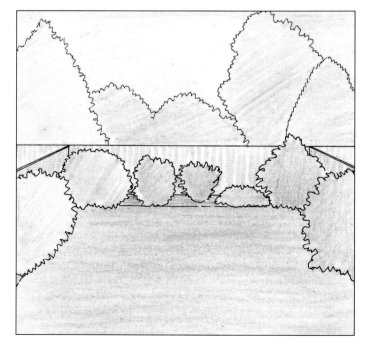

■ **ABOVE LEFT AND ABOVE RIGHT**
A small garden will seem box-like if the boundary is clearly visible, especially if it is plain and man-made like a fence or a wall, and the boundary will dominate. Simply adding a narrow border with masking shrubs will not help because the boundary, although better clothed, will still be obvious. Bringing the border into the garden in broad sweeps, with a hint of the lawn disappearing behind a sweep towards the end of the garden, will blur the boundaries, giving the impression of more garden beyond.

■ **ABOVE LEFT AND ABOVE RIGHT**
Straight lines can be uncompromising, and a dominant feature at the end of a straight path will foreshorten the visual appearance. Curving the path slightly, and perhaps tapering it a

little towards the end, will create the illusion of greater depth. If the focal point is also diminished in height or stature, the optical illusion will be increased.

■ **ABOVE LEFT AND ABOVE RIGHT**
A long, straight path will take the eye to the boundary unless the garden is very large, so try to introduce a feature that will arrest the eye part of the way along the path. A curve around an ornament, a large shrub or small tree will keep the eye within

the garden. If you do not want to move an existing path, try erecting an arch over it, planted with an attractive climber to soften the outline and perhaps extended along the length of trellis on either side.

PREPARING A PLANTING PLAN

The hard landscaping described so far in this chapter acts like a skeleton and gives the garden structure, but it is the choice of plants that gives shape and character to a garden. It's important to think about structure first, but getting the planting plan right is equally important if your garden is to have real impact throughout the year.

CREATING THE OUTLINE

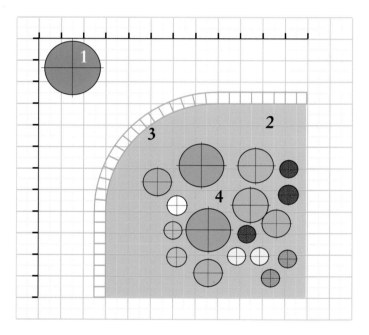

Start with the outline of the area to be planted, with distances marked on the graph paper to make positioning easier. Some good plant catalogues and books include plenty of pictures, and give likely heights and spreads for the plants. Treat heights and spreads with caution, however, as much depends on where you live, as well as on climate, soil and season.

If your plant knowledge is good, you may be able to draw directly on to your border plan, but if you find it easier to move around pieces of paper than use a pencil and eraser, cut out shapes to represent the plants that you are planning to include. Write on their height, spread and flowering period if this helps, and indicate their name on the back. Try colouring them, perhaps using stripes for variegated plants, and using green for evergreens. This will help form an overall picture.

KEY TO PLAN

1 Existing flagpole cherry (*Prunus* 'Amanogawa')
2 Lawn
3 Mowing edge
4 Cut-out plant symbols to position in border

ADDING THE PLANTS

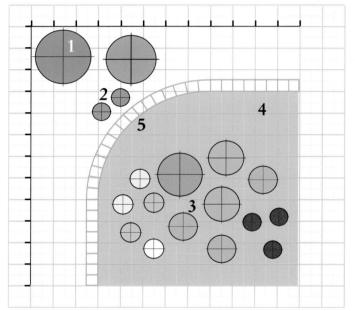

Position the symbols on your plan, starting with tall or key plants. It may be necessary to adjust them as other plants are added, but it is important that the key focal-point plants are well positioned as they will probably dominate the bed or border. Bear in mind the flowering periods, and ensure that evergreens are well distributed rather than clumped together, leaving large areas that will be bare in winter.

KEY TO PLAN

1 Existing flagpole cherry (*Prunus* 'Amanogawa')
2 Plants in position
3 Plants still to be positioned
4 Lawn
5 Mowing edge

FILLING OUT THE DESIGN

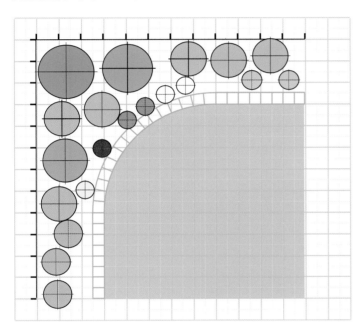

COMPLETING THE DESIGN

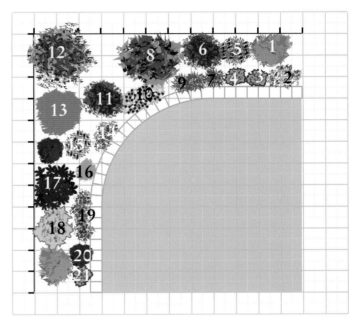

After placing the key plants, including tall ones best placed towards the back of the border, add the mid-height plants, but make sure some of these appear to drift towards the back of the border between the taller ones, to avoid a rigid, tiered effect. Finally, fill in with low-growing plants. The larger the drift of these, the more effective they are likely to be. Individual small plants often lack impact, and can be swamped by more vigorous neighbours.

The initial plans can be fairly crude as they merely explore the possibilities of various combinations and associations. To visualize the final effect more easily, draw your final planting plan in more detail.

KEY TO COMPLETING THE DESIGN PLAN

1 *Perovskia atriplicifolia* 90cm/3ft
2 Bergenia (evergreen) 30cm/1ft
3 *Diascia barberae* 30cm/1ft
4 *Houttuynia cordata* 'Chameleon' 30cm/1ft
5 Kniphofia 120cm/4ft
6 Rosemary (evergreen) 120cm/4ft
7 *Artemisia* 'Powis Castle' 90cm/3ft

8 *Choisya ternata* (evergreen) 120cm/4ft
9 Dwarf Michaelmas daisy 60cm/2ft
10 Cistus 45cm/1½ft
11 *Cornus alba* 'Sibirica' 120cm/4ft
12 Existing flagpole cherry (*Prunus* 'Amanogawa') 10m/30ft
13 *Camellia* 'Donation' (evergreen) 200cm/6ft

14 Agapanthus 75cm/2½ ft
15 Hosta 45cm/1½ft
16 Bergenia (evergreen) 30cm/1ft
17 *Anemone* x *hybrida* 75cm/2½ft
18 *Potentilla* 'Princess' 75cm/2½ft
19 Lavender (evergreen) 30cm/1ft
20 *Stachys byzantina* (almost evergreen) 30cm/1ft
21 *Mahonia* 'Charity' (evergreen) 240cm/8ft

LOW-MAINTENANCE GARDENS

Low-maintenance gardens can be high on impact, and they can be just as stylish as gardens that demand regular attention.

This style of gardening is great for busy people who want a stunning garden but simply don't have the time or inclination to devote to regular watering or mowing, or routine chores like weeding and deadheading. Anyone with a disability, infirmity or simply suffering the effects of age will also be tempted by the appeals of low-maintenance gardening.

With low-maintenance gardens, you should be able to go on holiday for a week or more and come back without apprehension. They can fend for themselves for long periods. These are gardens where most of your time is spent relaxing rather than working.

■ ABOVE
Paving is low-maintenance, but it needs plenty of plants to soften the effect.

■ OPPOSITE
This strongly patterned design shows excellent use of line and form, mass and void – all elements of good design. A few select evergreen plants are used to create the maximum effect with the minimum of effort.

INSPIRATIONAL IDEAS

Low-maintenance gardens are often created using only a few striking plants, yet it is also possible to have a garden full of plants. It is the choice of plants as much as the number that determines how much time you need to lavish on them.

■ **ABOVE**

Gravel and stone gardens are low-maintenance, especially if you plant them with drought-tolerant plants such as lavenders. A few plants go a long way in this kind of garden, and maintenance is limited to trimming back any plants that begin to outgrow their space. This garden was created by Hilliers for the Hampton Court Flower Show, England, and has swirls of different-coloured gravel for extra effect: in your own garden,

subject to regular foot traffic, you may prefer to use only one kind of gravel.

Weeds should not be a problem if the gravel is laid thickly. A plastic sheet laid over the ground first will prevent deep-rooted perennial weeds becoming a problem. Where necessary, it's possible to plant through the plastic sheet by making slits in the appropriate place with a knife.

■ ABOVE

Sometimes being big and bold within a small area can be extremely effective. Apart from the paving and brick raised bed, this garden contains little more than some large pots and plenty of pebbles and boulders. The use of large plants like *Phormium tenax*, arundinaria (a bamboo), and even a larch (larix) tree, provides plenty of impact. The use of a little colour, like the red nicotianas at the back, works all the better for being set among the greenery.

The choice of a bamboo fence gives the plants sufficient light for good growth while ensuring a good degree of privacy.

■ LEFT

You don't need a large space for a big impact. A small walled area can look stunning if the design is bold enough. Only a few different kinds of plants have been used here, but the varied textures of the garden floor compensate. The straight lines of the decking create an effective contrast with the organic shapes of stone and gravel. Mainly tender plants have been used in this dry garden, which is also a sun-trap. Most of these, like the echeverias in the blue bed in the foreground, will have to be taken in for protection where there are winter frosts, as this is essentially a summer garden.

The use of colour, on the walls and the edges of the beds, combined with the warm tones of the gravel, make this a garden of pleasing textures, colours and shapes even without the plants.

INSPIRATIONAL IDEAS

Whether formal or freestyle, minimalist or packed with features, successful low-maintenance gardens need careful planning.

■ **BELOW**
Courtyard and enclosed gardens can be cosy and private, especially if surrounded by high walls. By keeping the central part open, an impression of space is given, but a strong sense of form and structure is essential to create a "designed" look.

A strong focal point helps to give a garden a sense of design: here a row of lion mask water spouts commands attention. A design like this can look stark without plants, however, so the planting needs to be strong. Potted trees and shrubs have been used to soften the effect while retaining a formal style. Bear in mind that plants in containers require watering every day in dry weather, so it's worth considering an automatic watering system to save on the labour.

■ OPPOSITE TOP

These plants will tolerate dry conditions and do not demand regular watering. As well as making a pleasing backdrop for them, the gravelled surface should suppress weed growth.

The daisy-like annual dimorphothecas are easy to grow and bloom prolifically. Succulents such as echiums and *Agave americana* 'Variegata' should be placed in a frostproof place for the winter.

■ RIGHT

This strongly patterned design shows excellent use of line and form, mass and void – all elements of good design. It was created for the Chelsea Flower Show, London. Granite slabs have been set into the fine gravel, but for economy paving slabs could be used instead. Roof tiles set on edge have been used to create a strong, unusual pattern. The blocks of low-growing box (*Buxus sempervirens* 'Suffruticosa') can be achieved in a short space of time if a generous number are planted close together. This may appear extravagant, as box is fairly costly, but very few other plants have to be purchased for this style of garden.

■ LEFT

In contrast to the rigid formality of classical gravel gardens, this dry garden evokes a wild landscape. The seemingly random placing of the rocks and the sloping site without visible boundaries are cleverly planned to suggest that this garden is free from the rigours of design. Lavender, santolina and grasses have been planted in between the rocks for colour and a change of texture.

Know-how
THE GARDEN FLOOR

Although it may be the beds and borders that provide the initial impact in a garden, it's often the "floor" of the garden – lawns and paved areas for example – that occupy the largest area. This has a huge impact not only on time if you have to mow a lawn, but also in visual terms.

There are lots of ideas for hard surfacing (such as paving, decking and gravel) on these pages, with suggestions for plant alternatives to grass. Ground-cover plants are also important "carpets" for suitable beds and borders. It's important to get this aspect of the garden right, as, initially, it will be the most time-consuming and costly part of planning your garden. Also, consider carefully how much time you have to spend on maintenance, as your choice for the "floor" will eat into your time, as will maintaining the borders.

■ OPPOSITE
DECKING Consider timber decking instead of paving. If suitable timber is used, and it is treated with a good preservative, it can be long-lasting, attractive and practical.
DESIGN TIP *Stain the decking a colour that suits your style of garden or ties in with the interior decoration in your home. Although there are limits to the colour range of wood preservatives, there are many appropriate wood stains that can be used on already preserved timber. The size and spacing of the boards, and their colour, all change the visual impact on the garden as a whole.*

■ ABOVE
GRAVEL The gravel surface is useful for suppressing weeds (a path weedkiller, very carefully applied, should control weeds for a season if they do become a problem because of inadequate preparation or because the gravel is not deep enough). A large expanse of gravel is not to everyone's taste.

Sometimes a mixture of gravel and paving looks better than either material on its own.
DESIGN TIP *Gravel can be enhanced with paving. Rather than position the paving slabs in straight rows or a regular pattern, try to introduce a sense of randomness for a more informal style.*

UNDERSTANDING GRAVEL

Gravel comes in many forms. Some gravels are angular, others have more rounded edges, they come graded in different sizes (the larger ones are more difficult to walk on, but very fine ones can also be a problem), and colours vary enormously. As well as grey, gravels can be shades of brown, red, almost green, and even with a hint of yellow. The colour of all of them changes depending on whether they are wet or dry when viewed, and whether in shade or sun. Very pale gravels can cause a strong glare in bright sunlight.

Coloured gravels are sometimes sold in plastic sacks in garden stores, and these may be adequate for a small area. If buying gravel for a large area however, have it delivered to your home in bulk to save on cost. If possible, obtain small samples of those you think might be appropriate and try them out in a small area in your own garden.

GRAVEL Gravel is an excellent "flooring" for displaying plants and pots to their best advantage. Coloured gravel can be used to co-ordinate with containers.

DESIGN TIP *Empty decorative pots, grouped together or piled up, can be surprisingly pleasing and avoid the almost daily chore of watering. Position them by or near plants.*

DON'T BE BORING

Large areas of the same kind of hard landscaping material will look boring. Be prepared to mix different kinds of paving materials, perhaps timber and brick, natural stone paving slabs and bricks, or concrete paving slabs broken up with small areas or ribbons of gravel.

■ **RIGHT**

PAVING Unless the area to be paved is very large, consider bricks or clay pavers instead of concrete paving slabs. You can create different images with different laying patterns – a herringbone design has been used in this picture. Bricks and clay pavers often have a "warm" appearance that goes well with plants. Always check with the supplier that the bricks are suitable for paths – some are not and may crumble after frequent wetting and freezing.

DESIGN TIP *Try to soften the edging of paved areas with plants that will cascade or spread over the edge – but avoid those that will encroach too far and may become a hazard underfoot.*

Know-how

ALTERNATIVES TO GRASS

Some gardeners enjoy the physical effort of mowing the lawn – it's a useful form of exercise – but even the most energetic may begin to resent the time it takes in summer, or be dismayed at the visual impact an unmown lawn has on the garden if cutting has to be missed for a week or two through holidays or simply other pressures on time.

All-paved gardens are an option for small areas, but are not to everyone's taste, and most of us instinctively want to cover a large paved area with containers to add colour and interest – a course of action that necessitates the even more demanding task of frequent watering. For many of us, however, only a green lawn can set off a garden, giving it a natural kind of softness and beauty, and an attractive feature all year round. If you simply must have a lawn, don't despair – consider one of the alternatives to grass.

With the exception of moss and the creeping thymes, occasional mowing or trimming with shears will be necessary for alternatives to grass. This will ensure low, dense growth, and keep the lawn looking smart and tidy, but it will be a less frequent job than for grass.

Chamomile will produce white daisy-type flowers if the plants are not trimmed, which some gardeners find detracts from the effect. The variety 'Treneague' is usually used for lawns as it produces fewer flowers than other varieties.

Don't forget that edges will also have to be trimmed occasionally to produce a neat finish and prevent the plants straying into neighbouring beds or borders.

■ **ABOVE**
MOSS This may be a surprising choice for anyone who regularly buys mosskillers to treat their grass lawn. But there are many kinds of mosses, and some are attractive in the right setting. Normal lawn grasses would not do well in this shady area, for instance, but the moss thrives.
DESIGN TIP *Use moss for a damp and shady area where grass does not usually do well. It's not easy to buy moss, so you may have to encourage wild mosses and be patient.*

■ **OPPOSITE**
CHAMOMILE Chamomile (*Chamaemelum nobile*, still often found under its older name of *Anthemis nobilis*) is a popular first-choice alternative to grass. It's readily available as plants, it looks attractive, and it's aromatic when walked upon. It also requires only infrequent trimming. It's not without its drawbacks, however, as it's not as tough as grass, and you won't be able to use selective lawn weedkillers on it (a problem that applies to the other grass alternatives too), so weeding can be tedious.
DESIGN TIP *Avoid using chamomile for large areas. It will be easier to maintain and keep weed-free if used for a small area like the one shown here, which is walked upon only for access to a sundial. It's not a good choice for an area of the garden that takes heavy traffic.*

■ RIGHT

CLOVER Clover may sound like an unlikely candidate, especially as many of us spend time and money trying to eradicate it from our grass lawns. However, anyone who has a lot of clover in their lawn will know that it often remains green for longer in times of drought, and it can make a dense, ground-hugging carpet. You'll need to mow it occasionally to remove the flower heads and to keep the growth tight and compact.

DESIGN TIP *Clover looks best as a small decorative area like the area shown here. It can create a lush-looking, ground-hugging carpet.*

BE PREPARED

Prepare the ground well before planting or sowing these grass alternatives, paying special attention to the elimination of weeds. Because the effective weedkillers sold for grass lawns cannot be used on these alternatives, hand-weeding will remain a chore until the plants are established and have knitted together to suppress new weed seedlings.

■ ABOVE

THYME Thyme is another popular alternative to grass for a small area, its aromatic leaves being part of the attraction. There are many kinds of thyme, however, and the bushy ones widely used as a kitchen herb are best avoided. The more ground-hugging *Thymus serpyllum* is a good choice. Here thyme is in flower, its purple blooms providing an attractive contrast with the granite path.

DESIGN TIP *Try using thyme for small areas near a garden seat, or allow it to meander between beds provided traffic over it will not be heavy. It is also attractive when used in combination with paving slabs: plant it in crevices between the paving.*

Know-how
IN PLACE OF CONTAINERS

Low-maintenance gardens often have large areas of paving or gravel, with ground-covering plants or shrubs in the borders. The temptation is then to use lots of containers to make up for the lack of seasonal colour otherwise provided by bedding plants and other flowers. Resist the temptation until you've first considered the alternatives.

■ ABOVE
PLANTING THROUGH GRAVEL
Instead of planting in containers to relieve a large expanse of gravel, plant directly through the gravel into the soil. Make sure the ground is well prepared in the planting area, so that the plants will grow strongly and require only infrequent watering. The plants in this picture need no attention at all, except for annually cutting back any that have outgrown their space.
DESIGN TIP *If planting through gravel, plant in bold groups, which will have much more impact than isolated plants dotted around.*

■ RIGHT
PLANTING THROUGH DECKING
Plants can be planted through spaces left in decking, just as easily as in a paved area. Although yuccas do not require regular watering, the greater depth of soil than that offered by a container will ensure a better specimen.
DESIGN TIP *If planning to plant directly into the ground, it's much easier to incorporate the planting spaces at the design stage, than to lift paving slabs or cut decking afterwards.*

HOW TO PLANT THROUGH GRAVEL

If planting through an already established gravel bed, pull back an area of gravel to expose the soil, then plant normally if the soil is fertile. If the topsoil has been removed during construction of the gravel bed, remove some of the poor soil and replace it with fertile topsoil or potting soil before planting. If the gravel has been laid over a plastic sheet, make crossed slits with a knife and fold back the flaps far enough to plant. Water well before returning the gravel around the crown of the plant.

■ RIGHT
**PLANTING
THROUGH A PATIO**
Instead of planting in a
container on a patio,
try lifting a few paving
slabs to make a small
planting area. Mainten-
ance will be cut down
to a minimum, and it
makes a more
"planned" feature if
worked into the
original design.
DESIGN TIP *Don't
leave the soil exposed, or
weeds will spring up.
Fill any exposed areas
with gravel and pebbles.
It will look more stylish.*

AGAINST THE WALL
Planting spaces left in paving
are much better than
containers for climbers,
especially large ones such as
wisterias and roses. Whenever
possible, leave a planting area
in the paving, then train
climbers against the wall or
fence. It may be possible to
build up the edge slightly with
bricks or walling blocks, to
make the planting area a more
positive feature, but always
ensure the soil does not come
too high and bridge the damp-
proof course in the brickwork
of your home.

■ LEFT
RAISED BEDS
A better way of
introducing plants to a
paved area than a
number of containers.
They usually hold a
greater depth of soil
than do pots or tubs,
so plants are less likely
to dry out, and it
should not be
necessary to water a
raised bed daily during
hot weather. Also, a
single raised bed will
have more visual
impact than a group of
containers.
DESIGN TIP *In a
small area, a bed that is
not elevated much
beyond the surrounding
ground may be as
effective as a taller bed
would be in a larger
area, but in this case
make sure the roots can
penetrate the ground.*

41

Know-how

ORNAMENTATION

If you love terracotta and ceramic pots, or simply enjoy collecting interesting or unusual containers, don't assume you have to fill them with plants. Display them as ornaments in their own right. Those with a classic outline and a patina of age are ideal. Ornaments of all kinds can be used to give a garden that vital sense of "character".

FROST WARNING

Always check that terracotta or ceramic containers are frost-proof before leaving them out through the winter. Although empty containers are less prone to damage than filled ones, they can still crack or flake if not suitably fired when they are manufactured.

■ RIGHT
RUGGED ROCK
Areas of ground
cover like this
patch of bergenia
can look a little flat
and boring. An
ornament can
often help by
providing height
and acting as a
focal point. In this
instance, a piece of
rock serves the
purpose admirably.
DESIGN TIP *Use*
ornaments to give
height to a flat
area or to act as a
focal point in parts
of the garden that
otherwise lack
sufficient impact.

■ LEFT AND BELOW
GRAVEL TRANSFORMED Low-maintenance surfaces such
as gravel and self-sufficient plants such as conifers can appear
monotonous after a while, as the picture on the left shows.
Experiment with a few ornaments – even a simple pot like the
one below can transform the scene.

■ OPPOSITE
ELEGANT RESTRAINT If you have
been seduced by a stunning terracotta
container, don't feel that you have to
plant it – you will be committed to
regular watering. Try using such
containers as ornaments in their own
right, perhaps in a shady position where
most plants would not thrive anyway.
DESIGN TIP *Although these containers*
are large, small ones will work just as well
if used where their size looks in proportion
to the surroundings.

Planning and Planting
PRETTILY PAVED

A town or city garden, especially if enclosed by walls, often looks more stylish if the emphasis is on structure rather than masses of plants. Wall-to-wall concrete paving can look harsh and uninteresting, but warm-coloured bricks, laid in a pattern, provide a pretty background for plants as well as a practical surface for garden entertaining.

PLANNING

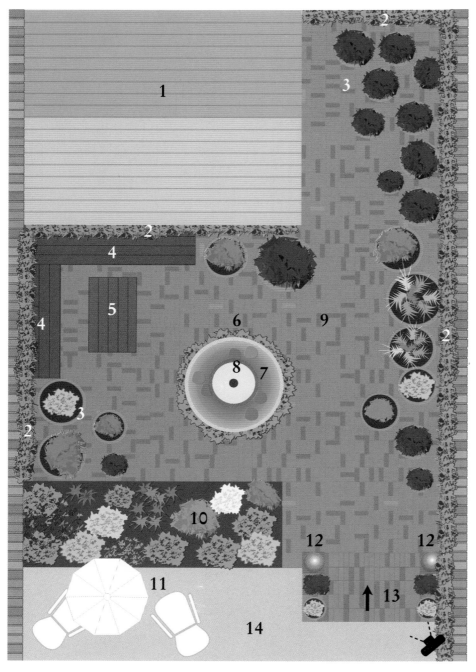

KEY TO PLAN

1 Garden shed
2 Climbers against walls and side of shed
3 Foliage plants in pots and tubs
4 Wooden bench seating
5 Table
6 Small-leaved ivy around edge of pool
7 Pool with waterlilies
8 Pedestal fountain
9 Brick paving
10 Shrub border
11 Sun-room
12 Stone finial
13 Brick steps
14 House

↑ Direction of steps down
↖ Viewpoint on photograph

This town garden demonstrates how even a simple design consisting of basic rectangles can be transformed by the use of suitable landscaping materials and plants into a superb garden full of charm and character. The bricks, laid to an attractive basket-weave pattern, give colour and warmth to what could have been a dull garden. A built-in bench makes the most of limited space, and using a circular pond rather than a rectangular one, as the rest of the garden might suggest, provides a larger area of paving and more walking space, especially around the sitting area.

The small size of the bricks in comparison with paving slabs, coupled with the extra area created by the circular pond, helps to give

PLANTING

the impression that the garden is larger than it really is.

The circular pond could be converted to a sandpit if you have small children, or it could start out as a sandpit and be made into a pond as the children get older.

The many containers have the potential of negating the time saved by not having a lawn. Even though shrubs that don't need daily watering during warm weather have been chosen in this plan, they still require regular watering. An automatic watering system is the best solution, otherwise it might be better to convert the standing area for the containers into shrub beds.

PAVING PATTERNS

The pattern to which bricks and pavers are laid alters the overall impression created when viewed en masse. Three common bonds are illustrated below. The stretcher bond is usually most effective for a small area and for paths. The herringbone pattern is suitable for both large and small areas, while the basket weave needs a reasonably large expanse for the pattern to be appreciated. Always confirm that the bricks chosen are suitable for paving – those intended for house-building may be unsuitable.

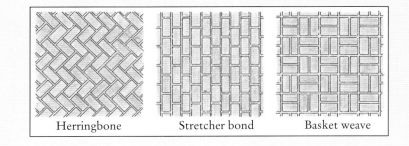

Herringbone   Stretcher bond   Basket weave

Planning and Planting
SETTING A STYLE

This low-maintenance garden uses granite setts to create an architectural tone, with a cabbage palm (*Cordyline australis*) as a centrepiece to add an exotic feel to regions where the winters are cool. Walling has been cleverly used to mask the garage.

PLANNING

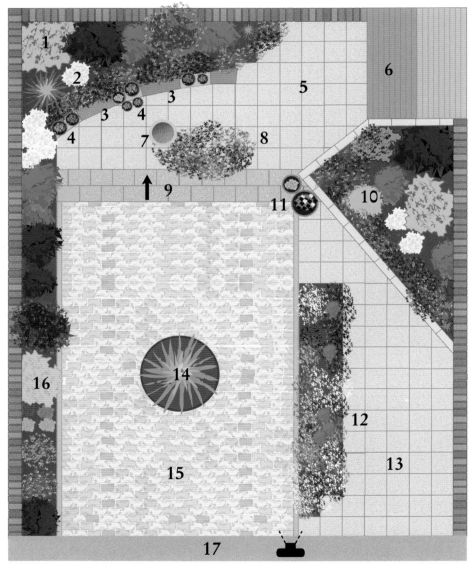

KEY TO PLAN

1 Shrubs
2 Ground cover
3 Seat
4 Plant shelf
5 Raised patio with slabs
6 Garage
7 Fountain
8 Low-maintenance shrubs
9 Steps
10 Low-growing shrubs and ground cover in elevated bed
11 Tubs with dry-tolerant plants such as pelargoniums
12 Alpines and low-growing border plants
13 Paving slabs
14 *Cordyline australis*
15 Granite setts
16 Shrubs and ground cover
17 House

↑ Direction of steps up

Viewpoint on photograph

In the absence of a lawn, a large area of paving can sometimes appear oppressive. In this garden, the paved area has been divided into three separate sections, with granite setts used in one for a change of texture, and a variation in height introduced to help break up the garden visually. Raised beds at the end of the garden are an effective screen to the garage.

In spring and summer months, low-maintenance shrubs and ground-cover plants ensure plenty of visual interest, but focal points, such as the fountain at the end of the garden, are essential to make this an interesting garden at other times of the year, when the plants have died back.

As this is an enclosed garden, the eye has to be drawn inwards, rather than out towards an attractive distant view, so an "architectural" plant such as a *Cordyline australis* is needed to provide a focal point and an axis around which the garden hangs. This plant is not completely hardy in cold climates, but it will tolerate frost, especially once established. In colder areas, a large *Yucca gloriosa* could be used instead.

PLANTING

CHOOSING PAVING

There are many more paving materials available from garden centres, builders' merchant and specialist mail-order suppliers than many people realize. Each type will bring its own colour and texture to your patio or paved area, so it's worth studying a variety of catalogues and visiting a number of suppliers before ordering.

Concrete paving slabs are perhaps the most widely used form of paving. The vast range of sizes, shapes, and finishes can make choosing a bewildering task, but bear in mind that many of the bright colours tone down with the effect of dirt, age and weathering, so finish and texture may be more important. Some have a finish that resembles basket-weave bricks, others resemble real stone slabs.

Clay and concrete pavers are often rectangular but come in other shapes. They are usually bedded on sand and vibrated in. Pavers fit together closely, whereas bricks have to be mortared, leaving a seam around each one. Bricks have the advantage of being available in many warm colours,

and it's easier to match the brickwork used for garden and house walls.

Stone setts, like the granite ones used in the garden illustrated above, create a strong sense of texture but may be a little more uneven to walk on. They mellow beautifully with age.

■ LEFT
The top row shows (from left to right) natural stone sett, clay paver, brick, artificial sett. The centre row shows a range of the different shapes of concrete paving blocks available. The bottom row illustrates some of the colours available in concrete paving slabs.

Planning and Planting

STUDY IN SYMMETRY

This is a town garden to sit and relax in, a place to meditate or relax rather than work in. Once constructed and planted, a garden like this demands little maintenance provided a self-watering system is used for the shrubs in containers, yet it's eye-catching and full of impact.

PLANNING

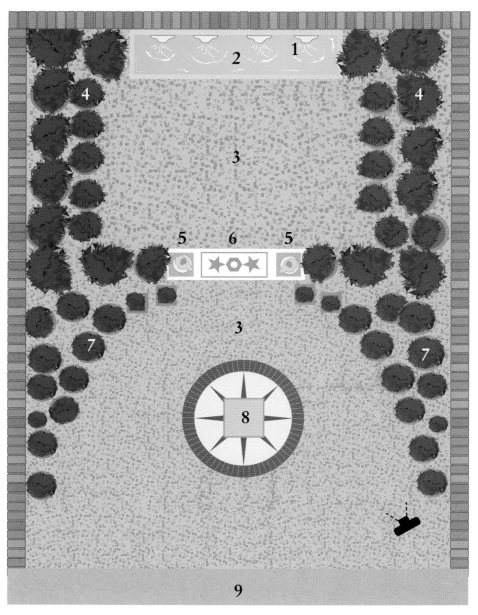

for their shape and texture rather than for an intrinsic sense of beauty or colour.

A sense of artistry is used in the mosaic paving that links the two parts of the garden and the floor on which the ornament has been placed. These strong visual images break up the garden so that the eye is arrested and there isn't a void in the centre.

Clipped box (*Buxus sempervirens*) emphasizes the formal style of this garden, and it is not especially labour-intensive to maintain. Two or three clips during the growing season will suffice to keep the plants looking reasonable – a few more trims will maintain a smarter appearance, but still less time and effort than the weekly mowing required for a lawn. Box are also reasonably tolerant if they cannot be watered regularly, but it's best to use an automatic watering system if possible. This will ensure the garden is truly minimum-maintenance, and the box will thrive that much better.

A very formal style like this depends on symmetry and bold features like wall fountains, mosaic, and matching statues to make a statement. This kind of garden will appeal to someone who enjoys shapes and a sense of order. Even the plants have been chosen

PLANTING

COLOUR AND SIZE

Gravels are available in many colours, depending on the rocks from which they were derived, and the grade or size also affects the appearance. Look around to find a gravel with an appearance that you like. Make sure you see it both moist and dry, because it can look very different.

HOW TO LAY GRAVEL

1 Excavate the area to a depth of about 5cm (2in). You can make the gravel deeper, but it means more soil-moving and extra cost.

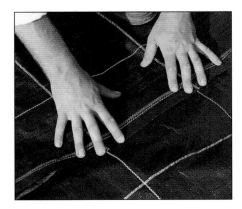

2 To prevent deep-rooted weeds appearing, lay a mulching sheet or heavy-duty black polythene (polyethylene) over the area, overlapping the strips by about 5cm (2in).

3 Barrow the gravel into position, then distribute it over the surface, making sure it is about 5cm (2in) thick. Use a rake to level the surface, then consolidate it by walking over it or rolling it. Re-rake if necessary.

Planning and Planting
FRAMING A FOCAL POINT

A dry garden like this benefits from a water feature such as a bubble fountain, which emphasizes the arid conditions all around and seems even more refreshing for that. Eye-catching structural features, like the moon gate and the ornament it frames, render the lack of bright plants unimportant. They give the garden high impact while still being low-maintenance, an impact that will be retained throughout the seasons.

PLANNING

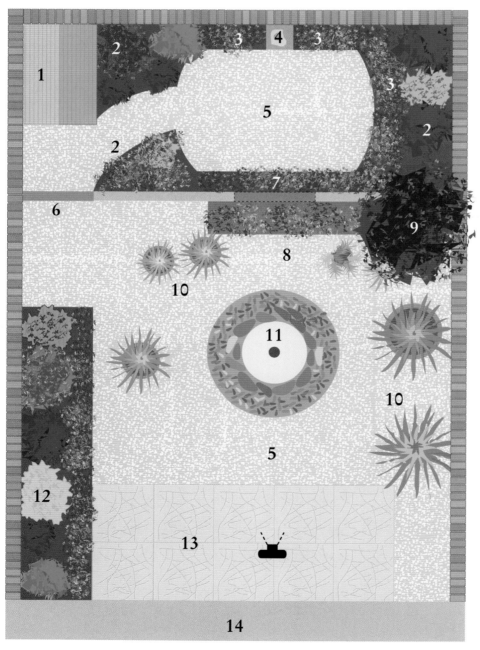

Dividing the garden into smaller sections is a good way to add interest and encourage a sense of exploration. In this garden plan, the construction of a wall with a marvellous moon gate, a circular hole built into the wall, not only provides an outstanding focal point but gives the impression of more garden waiting to be explored beyond the wall. The ornament positioned against the back wall ensures the eye is taken not only to the moon gate but beyond it, and the fountain in the foreground echoes and balances it. The yuccas and phormiums positioned in pots on the right-hand side help to frame the window in the wall and require less watering than most container-grown plants.

PLANTING

A WALL WITH A VIEW

As a design device, "windows" set into a wall have the kind of magnetic attraction that seldom fails to inspire favourable comment. If the view beyond is attractive, then they work well in boundary walls; where the view is less enticing, they are better placed within internal walls.

The options are limited only by your imagination, but most "windows" are rectangular, oval, circular or arch-shaped. The material from which the wall is constructed may influence your decision. Unless you have experience of bricklaying, it's best to employ a professional.

■ ABOVE
Viewing "windows" can be built even into natural stone walls. Windows like the one shown above were once a popular design feature for the end of a long walk or alley within the garden.

■ ABOVE
When the view beyond a walled garden is an attractive one, make the most of it! Here an elegant fountain is framed by a classic brick arch, surrounded with pretty yellow flowers.

Planning and Planting
IN PLACE OF GRASS

Sometimes an existing garden can be transformed into a low-maintenance one simply by replacing the lawn. This is especially worth considering if the physical effort of mowing is a problem as well as the time element. In this garden the lawn was simply replaced by gravel. The effect is a garden that retains its interest throughout the year.

PLANNING

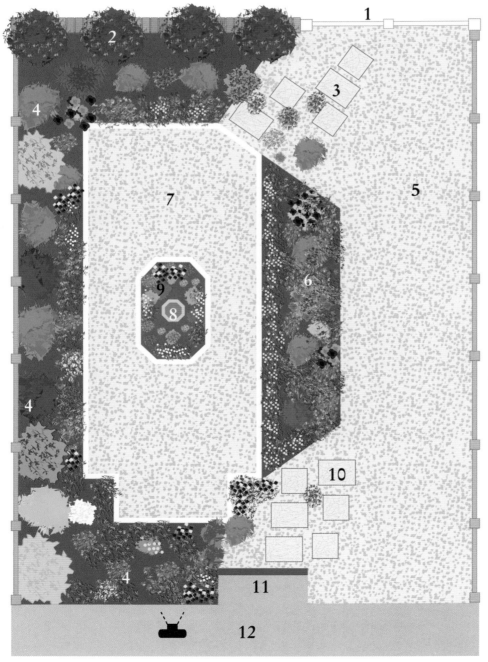

KEY TO PLAN

1 Picket gate
2 Conifers
3 Paving slabs and plants set in gravel
4 Mixed border
5 Gravel drive
6 Roses in mixed border
7 Gravel
8 Birdbath
9 Alpines and low-growing plants
10 Paving slabs set in gravel
11 Front door
12 House

▼ Viewpoint on photograph

Not everyone wants to be involved in a major redesign in order to reduce the amount of time and effort spent on the garden. It may be possible to change a few labour-intensive features, and the lawn is often a priority in this respect. Here it was decided to replace the grass with gravel. Even though weeding and dead-heading would still be demanding at times, it was mowing the lawn that was becoming a chore. The existing beds were left, and the grass lifted and replaced with gravel. To prevent the gravel spreading on to the surrounding beds, an edging was added to keep it in place.

IN REVERSE
If you consider that a garden simply isn't a proper garden without a lawn, but are not too concerned about lots of flowerbeds to look after, you could keep the grass and fill the beds or borders with gravel instead. This will also suppress weeds in the beds. To reduce the amount of grass to mow, it may be worth cutting some new beds into the lawn.

PLANTING

HOW TO MAKE A GRAVEL BED

1 Start by marking out the shape with a rope, hose, or sand sprinkled where the outline should be. Oval-shaped beds are ideal for small gardens.

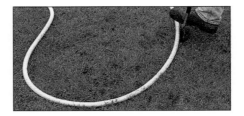

2 Cut the outline of the bed around the hose or rope, using a half-moon edger, or use a spade if you don't have an edging tool.

3 Lift about 10cm (4in) of grass with a spade. Add 7.5cm (3in) of gravel. Leave 2.5cm (1in) gap below lawn level to protect the grass from loose gravel.

4 For planting through gravel, fork in a generous quantity of rotted manure or garden compost, together with a slow-release fertilizer.

5 Allow the compost to settle before adding the gravel. Spread 5–8cm (2–3in) of gravel evenly over the firmed surface, and level it with a rake.

6 Gravel is best planted sparsely with a good space in between plants. Try adding a few stones or pebbles to enhance the effect.

Planning and Planting
CORNERING IN STYLE

Corner sites are always difficult to design, but if you can build a wall it's possible to isolate yourself in a very private garden.

PLANNING

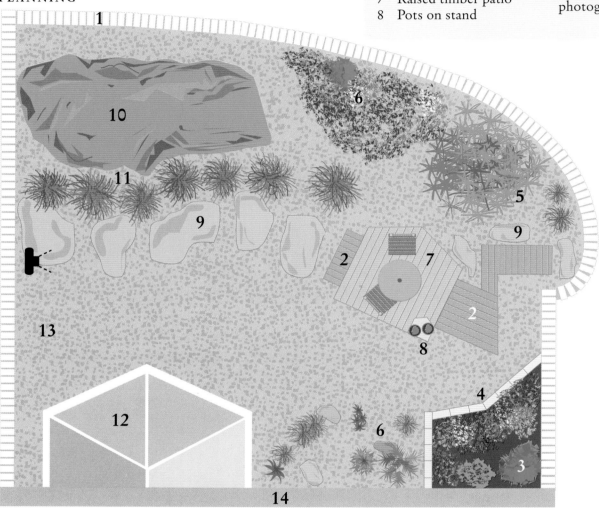

Here, a tall wall provides seclusion and privacy, creating an oasis in which a striking dry garden has been created. The white-painted finish helps to reflect light so that it doesn't look gloomy despite being enclosed.

In some places there may be restrictions on the height of wall that can be constructed in certain positions, mainly if they are likely to limit the view of traffic emerging from the road at a junction, so always check with the relevant authority if in doubt.

INEXPENSIVE GROUND COVER
Low-maintenance gardens often require lots of ground-cover plants to suppress weeds at the same time as clothing the ground. As they should be planted close enough to produce a carpet of foliage, a large number of plants are usually required. If gardening on a budget, keep down the cost by buying a few large plants and taking plenty of cuttings or dividing them if appropriate. Pachysandra is an example of an excellent ground cover that's easy to divide, even if the plant is still young.

HOW TO PLANT GROUND COVER

1 Ground-cover plants that spread by underground runners or have a crown of fibrous roots can be divided easily into three to four small pieces. Water the plant about half an hour before you start.

2 Gently knock the plant out of its pot. If it doesn't pull out easily, just tap the edge of the pot on a hard surface. It should then be possible to pull the plant without damaging the roots.

3 Carefully pull the root-ball apart, keeping as much soil on the roots as possible. Plants with a crown of fibrous roots can be prised apart into pieces using a couple of small hand forks.

4 If the crown is too tough to pull or prise apart with a fork, try cutting through it with a knife. If this is done carefully using a sharp knife, the plant should not be damaged too much.

PLANTING

5 It has been possible to divide this plant into eight smaller ones, but the number you will be able to achieve depends on the size of the original plant.

6 Replant immediately into the gravel or soil, if you don't mind starting with small plants. Otherwise pot up the pieces and grow them on for a year before planting out into the garden. Keep new plants well-watered until they are established.

Choosing Plants
LOW-MAINTENANCE PLANTS

Low-maintenance plants should not require attention more than once a year, and most trees and shrubs qualify on this score. Many play a more proactive role, by covering the ground with foliage and suppressing weeds – so-called ground-cover plants.

SUPER SHRUBS
Most shrubs are low-maintenance, but if you want to avoid annual pruning, choose evergreens, few of which require annual attention. *Viburnum tinus* flowers from mid-autumn to early spring, but it can grow tall and require pruning. Many hebes are compact and lots have attractive flowers, but some are vulnerable to cold winters.

Euonymus fortunei 'Emerald 'n' Gold' will grow in sun or shade, cover the ground horizontally or grow up a wall or the trunk of a tree, yet it's not so vigorous that it's difficult to control. Its striking variegated leaves will provide winter colour.

Hebe 'Purple Picture' is a good example of a low-maintenance shrub. It's evergreen, compact and rarely needs pruning. Like most hebes, however, it is not suitable where winters are severe.

SHRUBBY GROUND COVER
Ivy, though a climber, makes a good ground cover for shade, but more interesting are prostrate cotoneasters, such as *C. dammeri*, with red berries, the variegated forms of *Euonymus fortunei* and, of course, the many kinds of heathers (especially callunas and compact ericas). *Pachysandra terminalis* 'Variegata' produces a smooth carpet of green-and-white foliage even in dry shade.

BEAUTIFUL BORDER PLANTS
Choose border plants that do not require staking, are not prone to pests such as aphids or diseases like mildew, and do not spread so rapidly that they require frequent

Sedum spectabile will bring a border alive in autumn just as most of its neighbours appear to be dying back for the season. There are several varieties and hybrids, in shades of pink and red. These succulent-like sedums require practically no attention and do not need staking.

division. Pleasing all-round performers include astilbes, hemerocallis, kniphofias, and rudbeckias and *Sedum spectabile* for late flowers.

HERBACEOUS GROUND COVER
Although most non-woody ground-cover plants die back to the ground for winter, they are more likely than shrubs to have bright summer flowers, and they suppress weed growth in summer. Among the plants used for summer ground cover are hostas and geraniums such as *G. endressii*.

Hardy geraniums are popular border plants, and many of them make pleasing ground-cover plants for the summer. Although they die back for the winter, they are more colourful than most ground-cover plants when in flower. Geraniums come in a wide range of colours.

ALL-SEASON TREES
Most trees are low-maintenance, so it's really a matter of choosing what you like the look of and have space for. Good trees for medium or small gardens with a long season

of interest are ornamental crab apples (malus), hawthorns (crataegus), flowering cherries (various prunus), and small mountain ash such as *Sorbus vilmorinii*. *Acer griseum* is pretty and will still look good in winter with its cinnamon-coloured bark.

Acer griseum is one of several small acers that are unlikely to outgrow their welcome. They are slow-growing and well-behaved plants and look attractive in their dress of autumn colour. The cinnamon-coloured peeling bark makes an attractive feature throughout the year.

COMPACT CONIFERS

Dwarf and slow-growing conifers are great for low-maintenance gardens, but bear in mind that some will grow large or wide with time and some may eventually require moving. They form attractive "architectural" shapes, which can provide interest in sparsely planted gardens. There are narrow, upright growers, among the brightest being the golden *Taxus baccata* 'Fastigiata Aurea'; rounded shapes like the green *Chamaecyparis lawsoniana* 'Minima'; ovals like the golden

Thuja orientalis 'Aurea Nana' is a good choice for low-maintenance heather and conifer beds, with its golden foliage and oval outline, coupled with compact growth. It's slow-growing, usually reaching little more than about 60cm (2ft). The foliage turns almost bronze in winter.

Thuja orientalis 'Aurea Nana'; and prostrate ground cover conifers such as the 'blue' *Juniperus horizontalis* 'Bar Harbor'.

ALPINES FOR GRAVEL

Most alpines thrive in gravel, as the majority appreciate the good drainage. However, some alpines can be rampant and spreading, so

Armeria maritima, popularly known as thrift, is often grown in the rock garden, but it also makes a pleasing display when planted in gravel. Large areas of gravel are usually greatly improved by the introduction of plants such as this.

go for clump-formers such as thrift (*Armeria maritima*) and rock dianthus for low maintenance. There are many more ideal candidates, as well.

TROUBLE-FREE HEDGES

Hedges are excellent plants to define and give structure to a garden. However, many are tedious and time-consuming to trim, so avoid quick-growers such as privet (*Ligustrum ovalifolium*) or shrubby honeysuckle (*Lonicera nitida*). Give tall, fast-growing conifers such as x *Cupressocyparis leylandii* a miss too, as they will require a lot of maintenance.

Restrained hedges that demand little more than a single annual trim include *Berberis thunbergii*, beech (*Fagus sylvatica*), holly (*Ilex aquifolium*), and, for a conifer, yew (*Taxus baccata*) or *Thuja plicata* 'Atrovirens'.

Berberis hedges usually require clipping once a year, though for a more formal outline a couple of clips will improve the profile. Several berberis planted close together make pleasing hedges and form an effective boundary to a garden. They can also mask out noise or disguise unattractive features, such as a garage, refuse or compost area.

Patios, Balconies and Roof Gardens

No garden should be designed without a place to sit, and, although garden benches and attractive seats tucked away in an arbour or alcove are always inviting, it's worth including a patio or an area where a group can sit and relax together, and perhaps enjoy a light meal or a drink surrounded by the sights and sounds of the garden.

If your garden is very small, or virtually non-existent, a patio or even a balcony may serve as the garden, in which case it is your extra room, the room outside. Where there's space, patios offer plenty of design scope.

It's natural to place a patio near the house, which is practical if you use the patio for meals, but it doesn't have to be a rectangle placed directly outside the patio doors. You could angle the patio around the corner of the house. It doesn't even have to be close to the dwelling – the design may be more impressive if the patio is at the end of the garden, or even to one side.

■ ABOVE
A shady retreat for dining al fresco, combining natural wooden benches
with a sturdy stone table.

■ OPPOSITE
Where space is at a premium, a small curved bench can provide an attractive
sitting area. Position it where you can enjoy the fruits of your labours.

INSPIRATIONAL IDEAS

You should consider carefully whether you want a patio filled with plants and flowers or something more structural or "architectural", with few plants and a big impact. A successful patio is often an extension of the style of the house.

■ **LEFT**
Balcony gardens can be striking in their simplicity. This one is large and has the benefit of a solid wall, which offers privacy as well as shelter from wind. A similar style could be used for a patio if you have plenty of space in the rest of the garden to indulge your taste in plants. This design shows strikingly the effect of form and shape, and the design value of "void", an area left uncluttered by garden furniture or tall plants.

■ OPPOSITE

A contemporary garden for a warm climate. Tall cacti grow out of the gravel, and rocks and stones are positioned among the beds to add interest. This truly is a garden for relaxing and enjoying the sun. The black furniture suits the modern, minimalist style of the garden.

■ ABOVE

The style of this sitting area could not be a greater contrast to the white-walled balcony shown opposite, top. Here, the garden is wrapped around the seating, a kind of mini-patio tucked away within the main planting areas. This is not the kind of area suitable for entertaining or for the family to relax together, but is a cosier, more intimate, place where a couple can rendezvous, or two or three friends can relax to discuss the pleasures of gardening.

INSPIRATIONAL IDEAS

If gardening on a balcony, in limited space, you'll want to cram in as many plants as possible, but in a large garden with plenty of flowerbeds you may prefer not to be bothered by bees and insects attracted by flowers while you are relaxing or eating.

■ LEFT
A secluded sitting area surrounded by plants has a special appeal. It becomes part of the garden proper rather than an isolated patio. White-painted furniture helps to make a statement in an area that could otherwise become cluttered visually. The white-painted trellis also helps to make a visual boundary and creates the impression of a more designed and integrated area by picking up the colour theme from the white garden furniture.

■ ABOVE

In a large garden, an area like this makes an ideal, sheltered retreat. The overhead beams not only create the illusion of an outdoor room but also provide support for a variety of evergreen climbers. Although climbers provide a wonderful natural canopy, bear in mind that the support must be high enough for trailing shoots not to become a nuisance below. This is especially important if climbing roses are planted, as the thorns are a potential hazard.

■ RIGHT

Balconies can be exposed to the elements, and sitting on a balcony can be a public experience. Using plenty of plants, including climbers, helps to overcome these problems, and from a gardening viewpoint transforms a barren area of paving into a haven of beauty. Here, vertical curtains of green have been achieved by planting climbers and wall shrubs against the dwelling wall, and by fixing a climbing frame to the edge of the balcony.

Know-how
SOMEWHERE TO SIT

Gardens should be places to relax in as well as to work in, and although a deckchair or lounger on the lawn is a good way to while away a few sunny hours, a patio or balcony garden room should be designed for relaxation and recreation, planned and furnished to become an enticing place to eat or drink al fresco.

No patio or balcony garden is complete without somewhere to sit, and the style and materials of the garden furniture used can have a profound effect on how the feature is perceived. No matter how cleverly designed and well constructed the patio, an inappropriate table and chairs can spoil the effect, while well-chosen seats and tables can make even a mediocre patio look good.

■ **ABOVE**
FOLD-AWAY CHAIRS Balconies pose a special problem as space is usually limited. Rather than normal garden chairs, consider directors' chairs, which can be folded to take indoors.
DESIGN TIP *Design a balcony garden so that there is good access and an area where several people can gather to sit together without fear of falling over plants or pots. This may mean grouping containers together into a few choice areas, but the impact will not be diminished.*

■ **OPPOSITE LOWER LEFT**
ALUMINIUM Cast aluminium alloy furniture has the appeal of the old cast-iron types that it replicates, with the huge advantage of light weight. This type of garden furniture is available in a range of colours.
DESIGN TIP *Greens and browns will blend into the garden, whereas white will stand out. Choose a colour that reflects the effect you want to create.*

■ **LEFT**
WOOD Informal wooden garden furniture like this blends in beautifully. Here, the seat is arranged much as it might be in an indoor room, which helps to give it the impression of being an extension of the home.
DESIGN TIP *Position your furniture to take advantage of the garden's colours, scents and view. A fragrant climber will add to your enjoyment of the garden as you survey your handiwork.*

■ BELOW

BENCH SEATS Bench tables with integrated seats can be reminiscent of public picnic places, but small stylish ones will banish any suggestion of lack of taste. This one has been varnished to keep its natural appeal, which makes it attractive as well as practical.

DESIGN TIP *Avoid placing a rectangular table at right angles to the wall or edge of the paving. It will probably look more pleasing if angled, like the one illustrated.*

■ ABOVE

NATURAL MATERIALS Cane and wicker furniture is not ideal for leaving out in poor weather, but it is usually light enough to be carried under cover. It is also a good choice for a balcony. This type of chair adds to the impression that your patio or balcony is just an extension of the home.

DESIGN TIP *White furniture stands out well from a background of plants. However, in a bright, sunny place with lots of paving and few plants, white can look stark. Choose a colour that's appropriate to the setting.*

MATERIAL MATTERS

Patio furniture varies widely in price and quality, and there should be something to suit every taste and pocket. The starting point, however, should be what looks right rather than a prejudice about a particular material or concern over price. It may be better to buy one really good piece of furniture rather than several cheaper pieces, but sometimes inexpensive furniture is perfectly adequate for a particular situation.

Plastics and resins are often dismissed, but some types make strong furniture that lasts well and is easy to wipe clean, stack and store. If those qualities, especially portability, are important, don't dismiss these materials.

Timber furniture is always a popular choice, but here you probably do pay for quality. Hardwood furniture that is well made to last for years is not cheap, and it can be heavy to move around. It will also require annual cleaning and treating with a suitable oil or preservative if its colour is to remain strong and bright.

Cast-iron garden furniture is still available, and looks right where a period atmosphere is being created, but it's extremely heavy to move. Cast-aluminium alloy imitations look as good yet are light and easy to move. They are worth the extra cost.

Aluminium alloy furniture is usually painted or coated in a special resin. White is a popular colour, but it shows dirt easily. Browns, greens, even blues, are colours that do not show the dirt so readily, and look stylish too.

Know-how
A SUITABLE POSITION

Be imaginative about where you position the sitting and outdoor dining area – it doesn't necessarily have to adjoin the house, and it doesn't have to be a conventional patio shape. There are many other options, and the possibilities are limited only by imagination.

■ **RIGHT**
CLOSE FOR COMFORT There's much to be said in favour of a patio close to the house – especially if you do plenty of entertaining. It is also convenient for watering containers from the kitchen tap, and handy for harvesting culinary herbs planted in containers.
DESIGN TIP *Angling a patio at 45 degrees to the building makes it that little bit more distinctive and takes full advantage of the sun as it moves around.*

■ **BELOW**

A SHELTERED SPOT This is a traditional patio, in a sheltered position close to the house. It is purely functional, but for many gardeners that's what's required, and in this country cottage setting it blends in with the rest of the garden. The slight change of level between paving and lawn helps to delineate the patio area.

DESIGN TIP *Choose a position that's sheltered from too much sun or rain, and not exposed to cold winds. Shade for part of the day is not a drawback, and is often welcome, but make sure that the patio receives sun for at least part of the day.*

■ **ABOVE**

THE CENTRE OF ATTENTION Few would think of a sitting area in the centre of the garden, but it gives the impression of a garden designed for, and built around, people. Tasteful garden furniture is essential in this position, as it will become part of the main focal point of the garden.

DESIGN TIP *Don't be afraid to be different. It may bring that special quality to your garden that makes it personal, individual and powerful in a design sense.*

■ **OPPOSITE**

A PERMANENT OASIS This distinctive feature packs all the punch you could wish for. It's been sited away from the house, where the garden can be viewed in its full spendour, and is positioned to take advantage of the sun during the afternoon. Its position in the centre of the lawn acts as one of the focal points of the garden. The lightweight seating is easy to move around when required, while the fixed table, with its special planting area in the centre, looks good at all times.

DESIGN TIP *Don't be afraid to make your garden look lived in, or to be daring when it comes to built-in furniture! It can be a gamble that pays off.*

OBSERVATION PAYS

It's important to get the patio position right, and what appears to be a good position when planned on paper may have serious shortcomings in reality. It pays to sit out in the garden a few times, on different days, and ideally at different times of year, to assess whether it's a comfortable position as well as one that works in design terms.

You will soon discover whether shade, drips from trees or chilling winds caused by a wind-funnel effect between buildings are likely to be a problem. It will also give a better idea of privacy – if you don't want to be overlooked, it may be necessary to erect a screen or reposition the patio. A wall or a hedge might provide a private or sheltered position, or a patio overhead of beams supported on posts may give a sufficient degree of privacy. These can all be worked into the design and should be incorporated at the planning stage.

Know-how

EATING OUT

A meal outdoors always seems to taste better than the same food served at the dining-room table. A barbecue may be a bit smoky from time to time, and there may be the odd wasp to contend with, but it's all so much more fun. It isn't necessary to design your patio with meals in mind, but if you plan to do a lot of eating out it makes sense to consider the practicalities.

PORTABLE BARBECUES

Built-in barbecues look stylish and give the impression of a well-planned garden, but where space is limited, they may not be the best solution. Portable barbecues that can be wheeled out for a particular occasion work satisfactorily, and some of the kettle barbecues (those with a lid that closes over the food) are inexpensive, colourful and attractive. If you are designing a built-in barbecue, add a storage cupboard if possible, and also somewhere to place plates and kitchen accessories. If buying a portable barbecue, you may wish to consider a trolley barbecue with sufficient surface space for serving.

■ OPPOSITE TOP

TWO-IN-ONE Almost anyone with a barbecue will tell you that it is an uninteresting feature when not in use. Why not transform it into a seat? Remove the grill and metal plate, brush away any ash, then slot in the wooden seat. Add a cushion, and the transformation is comfortable and complete.

DESIGN TIP *If you have a small garden, make every part of it work. Look for multi-purpose features like this barbecue seat, or use a portable barbecue that can be stored away when not in use.*

■ OPPOSITE BELOW

DESIGNING WITH LIGHTS Lights positioned under a tree will cast a subtle light for dining, as well as dramatic, enchanting shadows.

DESIGN TIP *Consider electric lighting at the design stage, so that it can be planned without dangerous trailing cables. Low-voltage systems are the safest, but high voltage lights are more powerful and safe if installed by an expert. However, the cost of laying mains cable electricity lines in conduit will be cheaper if close to a mains supply.*

■ ABOVE

BUILT-IN BARBECUE If outdoor entertaining is high on your list of priorities, a built-in barbecue and seating is worth designing into your patio. This is an unexciting feature when the barbecue's cold, but here a white seat helps to enliven what could otherwise be a drab corner once the guests have left.

DESIGN TIP *Build the barbecue in a position that is unobtrusive when it's out of use, and away from a fence or other potential fire risk. For the same reason, avoid a position near overhanging trees.*

■ TOP

CANDLES Patio lights extend the hours of pleasure to be derived from your patio, and allow you to enjoy warm evenings to the full. Candles and flares lend atmosphere to an evening in the garden, as do lanterns.

DESIGN TIP *Position candle flares and lanterns where their light will cast evocative shadows around the garden. Grouped together, they will provide sufficient light for an atmospheric meal. Never leave candles, flares or lanterns unattended in the garden.*

Know-how

LOOKING DOWN

The surfacing material for a patio is usually chosen after the basic shape and position have been decided, but never overlook the relevance of this important choice. It will make a difference to the image your patio creates. Mistakes will be expensive and hard to hide. There are many materials from which to choose, and dozens of combinations to experiment with; here are just a few.

■ OPPOSITE ABOVE

PAVERS Bricks and clay pavers are popular for small patios, and they look especially effective if combined with brick pillars and low retaining walls. Not all bricks suitable for building walls are appropriate for paving, however, so check with your supplier or use a suitable brick that's a close match.
DESIGN TIP *Terracotta pots look good with bricks or clay pavers, but try using a group of them together rather than dotting them around: this will have more impact and look less fussy.*

DECORATIVE DECKING

The way the planks are arranged changes the appearance of decking, as these eight variations show. Not all patterns are suitable for an irregularly shaped deck. Those that form a number of symmetrical squares are more appropriate for a rectangular deck.

If in doubt, try laying out various patterns before you cut and secure the timbers.

■ OPPOSITE BELOW

DECKING Timber decking is easy on the eye and harmonizes well with most plants. There are many decking styles, some of which are illustrated in the box above, and by using different wood stains or colours, even more effects can be created. It's advisable to experiment with a small area, or draw up a plan before buying and laying decking, to make sure that the pattern you like will suit the shape and style of your patio. Decking is also good for covering up uneven or irregular surfaces and will provide a sense of cohesion.
DESIGN TIP *Wooden furniture blends well with decking, but other materials can be used. If you are using trellis as a boundary to a decked patio, staining this a matching colour will help to produce a co-ordinated look.*

■ ABOVE

COMBINED EFFECTS Modern concrete-based paving materials and walling blocks mixed with brick can look pleasing and are especially useful where a modern image is desired. Don't be too tempted by brash colours, as they can look garish when new and weather to a muted colour anyway.
DESIGN TIP *Give an area of concrete paving an edging of bricks, clay pavers or tiles. It gives the paving a more definite edge and the contrast provides a clean, sharp look.*

■ LEFT

CONCRETE Don't dismiss concrete as a material. Concrete pavers can work well in the right setting. Here they blend with the concrete blocks used as seats.
DESIGN TIP *Consider how materials will blend with other features on the patio. Here, concrete blocks give the patio a modern image, but they might have looked incongruous with aluminium alloy furniture in traditional style.*

Planning and Planting
SOPHISTICATED COURTYARD

Quarry (terracotta) tiles can work better than bricks or paving slabs in a courtyard like the one shown here, as they help to create the impression of an outdoor room. A garden like this is very much an extension of the indoor living area.

PLANNING

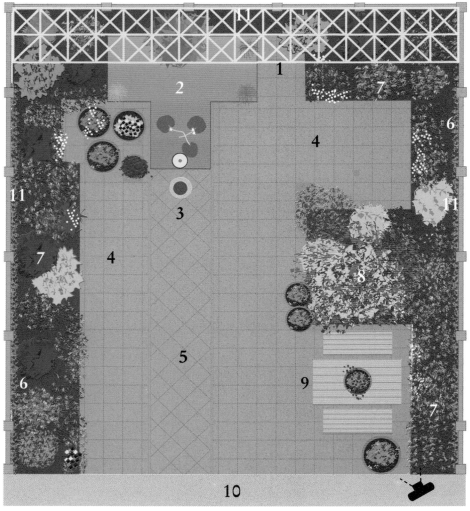

Here are instructions for building an upright trellis arbour, which can be adapted if you want to erect an overhead trellis.

CONSTRUCTING A TRELLIS ARBOUR

1 Gather together the trellis panels and "dry assemble" to ensure you are happy with the design. Two of the 200 x 60cm (6 x 2ft) panels are for the sides and the third is for the top. The two narrow panels and the concave panel are for the front and the 200 x 90cm (6 x 3ft) panel is to be used horizontally at the top of the back. Trim the wooden posts to length. They should be 200cm (6ft) plus the depth of the metal "shoe" at the top of the metal spike that will hold the post.

The type of paving used will set the tone of a patio or courtyard. These warm-looking quarry (terracotta) tiles reflect the warm-climate feel of this garden. Water plays an important role in this kind of design, but the formal pond does not have to be large, and a gentle fountain is more appropriate than a gushing water feature.

Even the most attractive paving can look overpowering if there's too much of it. Using a strip laid diagonally introduces the necessary visual break without damaging the sense of unity and harmony within the garden.

The long trellis overhead and the trellis enclosing the garden provide useful shade and a sense of privacy.

PLANTING

An upright trellis painted in a co-ordinating colour, and surrounded by colourful, fragrant plants in bed and pots, makes a perfect secluded retreat.

2 Start with the back panel. The posts need to be placed 200cm (6ft) apart. Mark their positions, then, using a club hammer, drive in a spiked metal post support (protect the top with a piece of wood or special metal insert). Drive a ready-trimmed post into each of the metal "shoes". Using the galvanized nails and the hammer, temporarily fix the top of the trellis to the top of the posts. Using a No. 8 bit, drill holes for the screws at intervals down each side of the trellis. Screw in the screws.

3 In the same way, position the front outside posts and fix the side panels, then the inside front posts and front panels. Fix the concave panel into the panels either side of it. Finally, fix the roof in position, screwing it into the posts. Paint the arbour with exterior decorative wood stain and leave to dry.

TOOLS AND MATERIALS

For a 200cm (6ft) long trellis:
Lattice (diagonal) trellis in the
   following panels:
   3 panels 200 x 60cm
   (6 x 2ft)
   2 panels 200 x 30cm
   (6 x 1ft)
   1 concave panel 200 x 45cm
   (6 x 1½ft)
   1 panel 200 x 90cm (6 x 3ft)
   6 timber posts 8 x 8cm
   (3 x 3in), each 2.2m (7ft)
Saw
6 spiked metal post supports
8 x 8cm (3 x 3in), each 75cm
   (2½ft) long
Club hammer
10 x 5cm (2in) galvanized nails
Hammer
Electric drill with No. 8 bit,
   screwdriver attachment
40 x 2.5cm (1in) No. 10 zinc-
   coated steel screws
2.5 litre (½ gallon) can exterior
   woodstain
Small decorating brush

Planning and Planting
SURROUNDED BY FRAGRANCE

Instead of making your patio formal and structural, try
building it into the edge of a border. You will feel more
immersed in your garden, and if you use plenty of scented
plants it will be a wonderfully fragrant experience too.

PLANNING

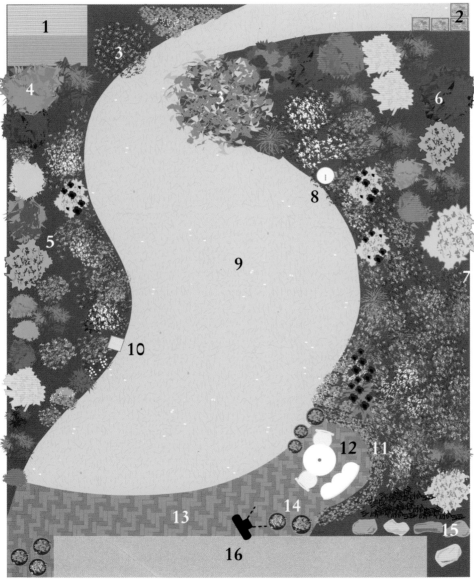

will enhance the aromatic delights
of sitting in this enchanting part
of the garden. Bear in mind that
these aromatic plants will also
attract lots of bees, which could be
an inconvenience.

SITTING PRETTY

Instead of buying garden furniture,
you could give some old tables and
chairs a lick of paint, and you may
be able to colour co-ordinate them
with the surrounding plants.
Wooden furniture will look best.
You can be sure of perfect toning
as paints are available in hundreds
of shades. If you don't have any
suitable old chairs, try junk shops.
To maintain the chairs in good
condition, keep them indoors
when not required outside.

If the formality of a rectangular
patio conventionally positioned
by the house does not appeal to
you, and you want your sitting
area integrated more naturally
into an informal garden style, try
building a small sitting area into
one of the borders.

The bank of thyme surrounding
the seating area will be fragrant
when touched or the leaves are
crushed, and the pots of lavender

PLANTING

These bright Caribbean colours may not harmonize with many plants, but your garden certainly won't be dull with a chair like this.

A combination of grey and white looks cool and elegant and will blend with most garden settings. Natural or muted colours contrast well with the bright blooms of seasonal flowers.

Prettily decorated with the bright colours typical of a summer garden, this chair would look wonderful surrounded by bright bedding plants such as fiery red pelargoniums.

The chair shown above blends in sympathetically with the painted shed behind. The delight of this project is that you can choose shades and colours to blend or contrast.

Planning and Planting
ON THE ROOF

Roof gardens have limited scope for radical overhauls as structural and load-bearing considerations will determine the scope. Furniture and plants are elements that will set the style.

PLANNING

Roof gardens offer more scope than balconies as they are often larger, but the problems are the same. The physical structure dictates the basic shape and limits of what you can do. Choose furniture and plants carefully to evoke atmosphere. Here, a formal garden has been created with box and other "architectural" evergreens in a simple planting scheme. These shrubs tolerate the winds more readily than less robust plants.

This roof is able to take the weight of the numerous clay pots, but with other roof gardens it may be necessary to use plastic containers and lightweight potting soil. Make sure they are heavy enough to withstand severe winds. If in doubt about your roof's load-bearing capacity, consult a structural engineer.

CLASSIC TOPIARY
Topiary is easy to maintain. When trimming, don't get carried away. Little and often with an ordinary pair of scissors is better than the occasional dramatic gesture with a pair of shears.

PLANTING

■ **BELOW**
left to right:
Ball topiary, corkscrew topiary, three-ball topiary and classic standard ball topiary. With patience and skill, box topiary can be trained from young plants. Buying ready-trained specimens will create instant impact.

POTTING TOPIARY

1 Knock the plant out of its original pot. Place into the terracotta pot containing broken crocks, and fill the space around the rootball with potting soil.

2 Push the potting soil down the side of the pot firmly, to ensure that there are no air spaces. Scatter the surface of the soil with plant food and water well.

3 To conserve moisture and create an elegant finish, especially on standard topiaries, cover the top with a generous layer of chipped bark or gravel.

Planning and Planting

CENTRE OF ATTRACTION

Your patio or sitting area will probably have far more character if you break with tradition and move it to a more central position, away from the house. A patio like this places you at the heart of the garden where you can admire the view.

PLANNING

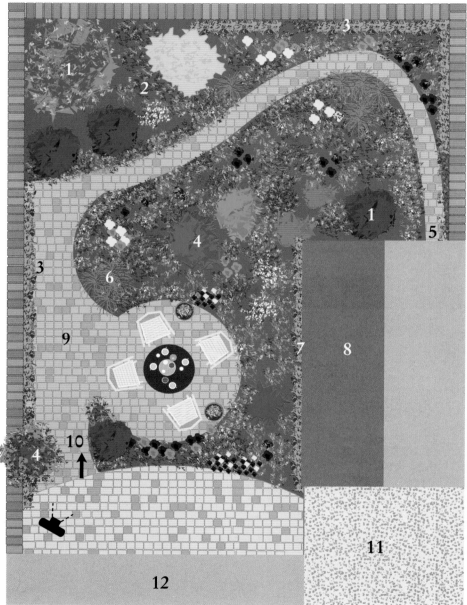

KEY TO PLAN

1 Specimen tree
2 Mixed border
3 Climbers on wall
4 Specimen shrubs
5 Rear door to garage
6 Mixed planting
7 Climbers on garage wall
8 Garage
9 Granite setts
10 Granite sett steps
11 Drive
12 House

↑ Direction of steps down

Viewpoint on photograph

The structure of this garden does not follow any of the common grids based on rectangles or series of circles, which amply demonstrates that design "rules" should be interpreted flexibly. Some of the best gardens give the impression of having simply evolved, with one part melting into the next. Curves and straight lines do not usually mix happily, however, and this garden is full of circles, arcs and gentle curves.

SITTING COMFORTABLY

Garden seats should be practical as well as pretty whenever possible. Charming and elegant seats are available in practical cast-aluminium alloy (they look like wrought iron from a distance, but are much lighter and more practical for use outdoors), but even old seats from around the garden and home can sometimes be renovated and used to give your garden character.

It is the clever use of meandering paths of granite setts combined with masses of plants that make this tasteful garden a delight for the plant enthusiast. Positioning the main sitting area slightly away from the house, so that it is surrounded by shrubs and mixed planting, makes it a magical place to sit and have a meal.

PLANTING

■ RIGHT
The old Lloyd loom chair illustrated had been given a new look a few years earlier with two shades of blue spray-on car paint. Even though the finish has become worn, the chair exudes a comfortable, cottage-garden feel. This kind of chair is not really weatherproof, but it can sit in a conservatory and be brought out for special occasions.

■ ABOVE
Metal benches are often unattractive, but this one was given a new lease of life when it was painted a bright Mediterranean blue. Used with a couple of co-ordinated cushions, it would add charm to any sitting area.

Planning and Planting
ELEGANT FORMALITY

Even city gardens like this one offer scope for a sense of spacious elegance, combining a long, open view to a distant focal point with plenty of interest-packed areas of restrained formality.

PLANNING

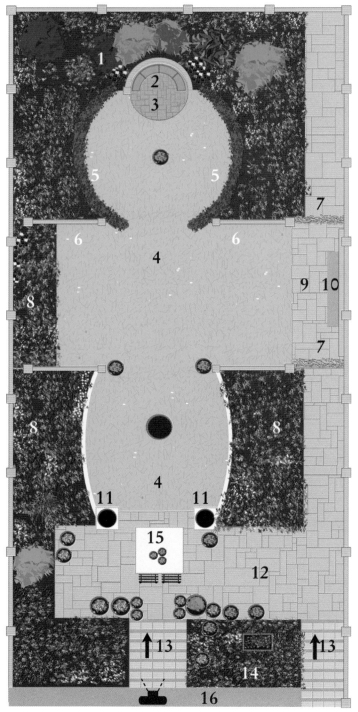

A design with many interesting features, this garden illustrates how effectively a simple device like a trellis can break up the garden visually. Shaped trellises have been used to divide the garden into a series of compartments. A trellis adds height and structure without blocking the view or casting a heavy shadow in the way that a hedge or wall does. Trellises can also be painted or stained in various colours to create a particular mood or emphasize a style.

It's possible to buy ready-made shaped trellises from specialist suppliers, but they can also be made to suit a specific need.

The curved trellis at the end of the garden encloses a small sitting area, something that balances the patio at the house end of the garden and also provides a focal point. It's a good idea to have more than one patio, so that you always have a sunny place to sit as the sun moves around. The secondary sitting area does not have to be large. This kind of design is easily achieved without a great deal of construction if there is already an existing central lawn.

PLANTING CLIMBERS
Trellises of all kinds, whether grand like the ones shown in the picture above or modest and erected specifically for a climber, demand to be clothed. It's not necessary to cover the whole trellis with climbers (sometimes the exposed structure strengthens the sense of design), but a good degree of cover avoids it looking too bare.

If the trellis is close to a wall or fence, it's very important to plant a little distance away, to avoid the worst of the "rain shadow".

PLANTING A CLIMBER

1 Excavate a hole twice the diameter of the rootball. The centre of the plant should be 30cm (1ft) away from the wall or fence, otherwise the roots will be too dry. Dig in a generous amount of rotted manure or garden compost, to help hold moisture in the soil as well as add nutrients.

2 Water the plant, then gently knock the bottom of the container to remove the plant from its original pot. Carefully tease out some of the fine roots from around the edge of the rootball, to encourage them to grow into the surrounding soil. Return the soil to the hole and firm.

3 Loosen the stems if they have been tied to a support cane in their pot, and spread them out evenly, spreading them wide and low. Tie in.

4 Water thoroughly after planting, and continue to water carefully until established. Apply a mulch to reduce water loss and suppress weeds.

Planning and Planting
SIMPLE ELEGANCE

Often simple shapes well executed have the most impact. This garden is based on rectangles around a large lawn. The patio is situated a distance from the house, linked by herringbone paving, which gives it a strong "architectural" element.

PLANNING

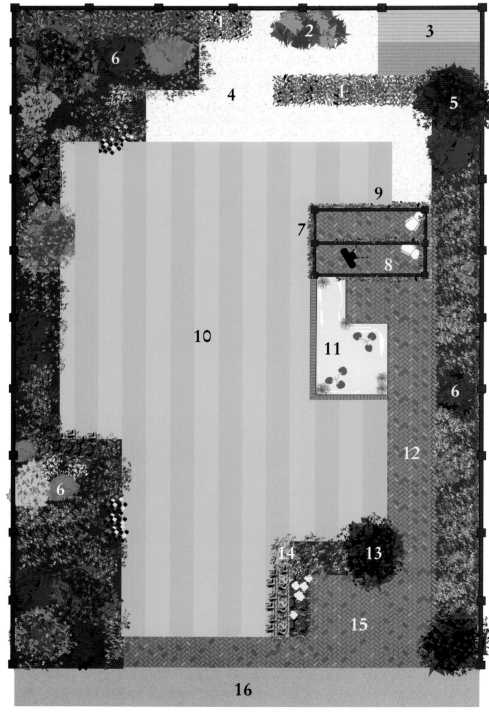

The choice of materials as well as the basic shape of the garden helps to create a sense of unity. In this garden, brick has been used extensively to link the various parts, and particularly the house and patio. Brick pillars for the patio overhead continue the theme and make the feature a more substantial element in the overall design.

Lighting has been built into the pillars as part of the patio lighting, to make this an area of the garden to be enjoyed for relaxing or dining after dusk as well as by day.

LAYING CLAY OR CONCRETE PAVERS
Bricks are usually bedded on mortar with mortared joints, but clay or concrete pavers are bedded directly on to sand. Their dimensions ensure they lock together simply by vibrating or tamping sand between them. They can be used instead of bricks, for patios or paths.

PLANTING

HOW TO LAY CLAY OR CONCRETE PAVERS

1 Excavate the area and prepare a sub-base of about 5cm (2in) of compacted hardcore or sand-and-gravel mix. Set an edging along one end and side first. Check that it's level, then mortar it into position, and lay the pavers.

2 Lay a 5cm (2in) bed of sharp sand over the area, then use a straight-edged piece of wood between two height gauges, notched at the ends so the wood strikes off surplus sand and provides a level surface.

3 Position the pavers in your chosen design, laying about 2m (6ft) at a time. Make sure they butt up to each other tightly, and are firm against the edging. Mortar further edging strips into place as you proceed.

4 Hire a flat-plate vibrator to consolidate the sand. Alternatively, tamp the pavers down with a club hammer used over a piece of wood. To avoid damage do not go too close to an unsupported edge with the vibrator.

5 Brush loose sand into the joints of the pavers with a broom, then vibrate or tamp again. It may be necessary to repeat the vibrating process once more for a firm, neat finish. The patio should be ready to use straightaway.

PATIO, BALCONY AND ROOF GARDEN PLANTS

The majority of plants can be grown in pots. Use shrubby and annual climbers to clothe patio walls, and a few striking "architectural" shrubby plants as focal points, but make the most of bedding plants, tender perennials and containers for masses of summer colour.

CLIMBERS AND WALL SHRUBS

Patios and balconies almost always have a wall boundary on at least one side, which would be more attractive if clothed with attractive climbers or wall shrubs. Ivies are ideal for clothing a large wall, but try to include plants with flowers or attractive berries to make it more interesting. Large-flowered clematis are ideal if supported on a trellis, but avoid rampant ones such as *C. montana*. Avoid thorny climbing or rambling roses if the space is confined. Pyracanthas are ideal wall shrubs as they can be trained and confined easily.

Clematis Large-flowered clematis are among the most popular and spectacular climbers to grow up a trellis. These varieties are 'Nelly Moser' (top) and 'Lasurstern' (bottom), but garden centres will have many to choose from.

"ARCHITECTURAL" SHRUBS

These are plants with a strong profile such as a spiky appearance or large bold leaves, which act as a focal point or a clearly defined shape. Avoid plants with spine-tipped leaves, such as *Yucca gloriosa* for example, as these can be dangerous, especially for children. *Cordyline australis* has a spiky appearance but softer tips, and there are prettily variegated varieties. Phormiums make striking plants for beds or large containers, and are available with variegated and coloured leaves.

Cordyline australis 'Albertii' is one of several variegated forms of this architectural plant, useful as a focal point. It is likely be less hardy than the all-green species, so it may require winter protection in cold areas.

BORDER PLANTS FOR CONTAINERS

Few border plants are used in containers other than hostas, but it's worth experimenting if you have spare pieces of border plants left over when you divide them. Because they are not usually grown in containers, the impact of potted border plants can be greater. *Lychnis coronaria* can be very pleasing, and *Ligularia dentata*

Hostas come in many forms. Most are attractively variegated, and some have pleasant flowers. They do surprisingly well in containers if watered regularly. This makes them highly desirable foliage plants for a patio.

'Desdemona' can be impressive with its large, almost purple leaves. Generally, foliage plants are a better choice than those grown mainly for flowers.

TREES AND SHRUBS FOR CONTAINERS

Patio colour is usually provided by summer-flowering seasonal plants, but it's worth growing a few evergreen shrubs in large containers, so that your patio or balcony does not look too bleak in winter. *Viburnum tinus* is especially useful because it flowers all winter. *Fatsia japonica* is grown mainly for its striking foliage, but mature plants do have ball-like heads of whitish flowers in late autumn. Small trees such as laburnums and some acers can be grown successfully in large pots.

PATIO ROSES

Most roses can be grown in large containers, but they will be much happier in beds beside the patio or cut into a patio. There are, however, patio roses – really dwarf and compact floribunda (cluster-flowered) varieties – that perform well in pots and in patio beds. 'Sweet Dream' and 'Top Marks' are particularly good, but there are many more.

Patio roses do best in flowerbeds or raised beds on the patio, but will usually put on a respectable performance in a container too. This one is 'Top Marks', one of the most highly regarded varieties among professional rose growers.

POPULAR BEDDING PLANTS

Any of the popular bedding plants can be used in patio containers, and which you grow is purely a matter of personal preference. Pelargoniums (bedding geraniums) should be on the short list, however, because they have that Mediterranean look and thrive in a hot position. They are also less demanding regarding watering than most other bedding plants. Busy Lizzies (impatiens) are also priority patio plants because they

Trailing pelargoniums, with their bright, vigorous blooms, can be used to great effect in both window boxes and hanging baskets. They are particularly good plants for containers as they will tolerate a period of dry soil better than most plants.

are so long-flowering and tolerate shade or sun. The New Guinea hybrids, which have larger flowers and sometimes variegated leaves, are not generally used for mass bedding, but they make excellent patio plants.

INTERESTING TENDER PERENNIALS

The group of brightly coloured summer flowers loosely called tender perennials, to distinguish them from bedding plants raised from seeds, are always worth including. They have to be propagated vegetatively and overwintered in a frost-free place, so if you don't have a greenhouse it's usually necessary to buy fresh plants each year. Fuchsias are a popular example, but try some of the bright daisy-like plants too, as these suggest a warm climate. Argyranthemums, venidioarctotis, and osteospermums are good examples and will continue flowering over a long period.

Argyranthemum frutescens is probably still better known as *Chrysanthemum frutescens*. There are many varieties with daisy-like flowers in shades of pink, yellow and white, produced over a long period. This is is 'Sharpitor'.

A TOUCH OF THE EXOTIC

A sheltered patio or balcony may provide the right environment for some of the plants more usually grown in a greenhouse or conservatory, where winters are frosty. Coleus are easily raised from seed, so can be discarded at the end of the season. Try putting some of your houseplants on the patio for the summer, after careful hardening off (acclimatizing).

Coleus are often grown as pot plants, but they can be grown very successfully in the garden. They are easy to raise from seed, started into growth in warmth in mid or late winter.

THE JAPANESE INFLUENCE

Authentic Japanese gardens are constructed according to strict rules, and features carry a significance that is seldom appreciated by Westerners. This in no way detracts from our ability to enjoy the style and aesthetics, and to incorporate some Japanese features into our own gardens, even if they lack the underlying significance of "authentic" Japanese gardening.

Whole books are written on the subject of Japanese gardening, but most of our designs seek only to capture the mood. Gardens have to be adapted to suit the environment and culture in which they are built. In our Western gardens, we may wish to introduce the Japanese influence only into part of our garden, or use a few key features as garden ornaments. Japanese votive lanterns, for example, are widely bought and positioned without regard to their original significance and are enjoyed purely as attractive garden ornaments. On the other hand, an area set aside as a Japanese-style garden will have a sense of peace and tranquillity that's special and supremely relaxing. Even if you are not persuaded to convert the whole of your garden, a Japanese corner will certainly add grace and elegance.

■ ABOVE
A simple feature like this evokes images of Japanese culture.

■ OPPOSITE
A Western interpretation of the style, using Japanese features and plants.

INSPIRATIONAL IDEAS

Japanese influences can be introduced to your garden in varying degrees. You won't have to completely redesign your garden for it to take on an oriental air. A bamboo screen, fountains, or lanterns can all add to the effect if chosen and positioned with care.

■ OPPOSITE

The space at the side of a town house is often neglected because it's so difficult to persuade plants to thrive there, and the scope for a strong design is severely limited. This design shows how Japanese images and features can be put to good use in a most unpromising position. Note the use of bamboo and reed screens to help mask the surroundings, which would certainly have lessened the impact of this type of garden.

■ BELOW

A garden like this won't demand much maintenance, other than clipping the domes two or three times a year, yet it has as much impact as one packed with flowers. This genuine Japanese garden may not be to the taste of gardeners more used to a rainbow of colour and a garden packed with as many different kinds of plant as possible, but it has a different function.

■ BELOW

Although there are Japanese influences in the water garden, this is clearly a hybrid with a more traditional Western style. For many gardens, this may work better than a stricter interpretation of the Japanese style.

INSPIRATIONAL IDEAS

The starkness of Japanese-style gardens may be unappealing to gardeners who expect to see greenery and colourful blooms. However, as these pictures show, the appeal of natural materials compensates with a serene style, which often requires the minimum of care.

■ **LEFT**
This is typical of a garden where elements of Japanese gardening have been mixed with normal Western elements, without attempting to follow authentic Japanese gardening philosophy. There's nothing wrong with this, as any garden should reflect personal preferences, which may involve borrowing from many styles.

■ **BELOW**
In a small or town garden it may be possible to devote only a corner to a collection of Japanese images. This inevitably means compromises, but the message is received clearly even in this small corner. It has been helped by creating a background that doesn't detract from the illusion. Painting the brickwork white helps enormously, and the bamboo fence is infinitely better than the traditional wooden fence that was probably there before the transformation.

■ **OPPOSITE**
Though created far from Japan, this garden shows strong oriental influences. The surrounding fences and buildings could have killed the illusion, but reed screens have been used cleverly to mask a potentially distracting background, and they make an uncluttered backdrop against which to view the various features to advantage.

Know-how
THE MAGIC OF LANTERNS

You don't have to be a student of authentic Japanese garden design to use and appreciate many of the features associated with this style of garden. Votive lanterns can be used as attractive ornaments if you are content not to look for deeper significance. Specialist catalogues offering lanterns and features such as deer scarers and water basins may use the Japanese names, but you will be understood if you ask for them by their English equivalent.

Lanterns are widely used in Western gardens merely as garden ornaments, but in traditional Japanese gardens the different kinds each have a particular significance, and they are always positioned with great care. If they are used as ornaments, however, do not be afraid to position them where they look pleasing.

■ **LEFT**

POSITION Make the most of winding paths in a large garden by positioning lanterns to show the way. Lanterns were used to light the way to an evening tea ceremony or to draw attention to a particular scene.

DESIGN TIP *Small Japanese acers and moss-covered ground will emphasize the oriental theme. Avoid plants that might look alien in a traditional Japanese garden.*

■ **BOTTOM**

PAGODA-SHAPED LANTERNS

Kasuga-style lanterns, with their pagoda-shaped tops, are named after a shrine in Nara, Japan. They make a bold focal point and can often dominate the scene.

DESIGN TIP *Position the lantern at the edge of a pond if possible so that its long reflection is cast across the still water for a dramatic effect.*

■ **OPPOSITE ABOVE**

PEDESTAL LANTERNS *Rankei*-style lanterns are set on an arching pedestal so the light extends out over the water, the better to reflect the image.

DESIGN TIP *Position the lantern so that it looks pleasing close up but also so that it forms a focal point across the water, at a distance or from another part of the garden. By giving careful consideration to positioning, it's usually possible to achieve both these aims.*

■ **OPPOSITE BELOW**

SNOW-VIEWING LANTERNS

Yukimi-doro or snow-viewing lanterns are often placed close to water. This position is used because when snow covers the wide top and the lamp's light reflects on the water, the effect can be particularly beautiful. The large roof also represents the shape of a Japanese farmer's rush hat. Lanterns were traditionally used near bridges to light the way.

DESIGN TIP *Lanterns, bridges, water, rocks, and gravel are all strong elements in Japanese gardens, so if space is limited try to introduce them in close proximity if possible. Do not cram in so many elements that it looks cluttered, however, as a sense of space is equally important.*

BUYING AND FIXING LANTERNS

Top-quality stone lanterns, made from materials such as granite, are expensive and heavy to handle. Consult specialist suppliers, and take your time choosing. Consider where you will be placing the lantern before you order.

Genuine stone lanterns are heavy and are likely to be shipped from Japan in sections. It's important that these are fixed together securely for safety reasons. Follow the suppliers' advice on assembly and fixing materials.

Reconstituted stone versions are cheaper, but perfectly adequate if viewed from a distance, perhaps across a lake or pond.

Lightweight resin reproductions are surprisingly good and perfectly adequate for a budget garden.

Lanterns should strictly be positioned at certain critical angles, to your home for instance, but your specialist supplier should be able to offer advice if you desire to lay out your garden in an authentic Japanese design.

Know-how
WATER FEATURES

Ponds, lakes and streams form the heart of many large Japanese gardens, but in a small garden the scope for these may be limited.

Fortunately, water is used in many other ways, most of which can be incorporated into even a modest-sized garden.

■ LEFT

DISPLAY PLATFORMS You can make a small pond look oriental if it's accompanied by suitable bridges and rocks. Here, a couple of charming bonsai, displayed on a platform that reflects the materials and style of the bridge, bring out the essential "Japanese" ambience.

DESIGN TIP *Don't use rocks only around the edge of the pond. Try to position a few rocks in the water as well. Try covering them with moss and perhaps planting a bonsai in a suitable crevice. Be careful not to puncture the liner (use pieces of off-cuts beneath the rocks), and don't forget that your bonsai will still require regular watering despite being surrounded by water.*

■ RIGHT

WATER BASIN
Water basins capture the essence of a Japanese garden, and are small enough to feature in any garden. Traditionally, the water is fed through a bamboo flume.

DESIGN TIP *Don't be tempted to elevate the basin higher than suggested by the manufacturer. The low-level placement is symbolic, requiring a low stooping position to use it, as a gesture of humility for the ritual cleansing before the tea ceremony.*

■ LEFT

BRIDGES Water provides an ideal excuse for including a wonderful Japanese bridge, bright red being the usual colour. These are focal points in their own right, but also cast enchanting reflections.

DESIGN TIP *Whether making the bridge or buying it, it makes sense to span the narrowest part of the pond or stream. If necessary, just make a small inlet that extends a little way past the bridge to give the illusion that the water flows beyond.*

PUMPS

Most small water features, such as deer scarers and water basins, require only a very gentle flow of water. An inexpensive, small, low-voltage pump is adequate, and this can be housed in a small hidden reservoir beneath the feature, water trickling through pebbles supported on a strong mesh base, to be recirculated.

■ RIGHT

ORNAMENTS This large pond benefits from this focal point. Ornaments should be simple but striking, and have relevance to the scene.

DESIGN TIP *Don't overdo the ornaments, especially if you have used lanterns around the garden. Too many focal points will clash with each other. A few striking features usually work better than many mediocre focal points.*

Know-how

ROCK AND STONE

From early times, the Japanese have had a deep and abiding affinity with rock. Rock forms an important element in their landscape, and it symbolizes durability. It is possible to construct a Japanese garden without rocks, but it would be a pity not to include this most attractive of materials.

■ **BELOW**
CHOOSING ROCKS Consider colour, texture and size when choosing rocks. Here the different surfaces and sizes look as though they have been deposited naturally beside the stream. DESIGN TIP *Random positioning of rocks and pebbles will create a natural look, enhanced by clusters of water plants.*

■ ABOVE
LARGE ROCKS A couple of large rocks have transformed a potentially dull corner of this Japanese garden. Whether you view them as symbols or simply as an ornament, they are a striking focal point and make a feature of a part of the garden that would otherwise go almost unnoticed.
DESIGN TIP *Rocks like this are heavy to move. To help get the positioning right without too many attempts, make a number of sketches to show the selected rocks in a number of positions. Begin to position them only when you have a sketch that looks convincing.*

■ BELOW
FEATURE FOUNTAIN A drilled boulder through which water is pumped so that it trickles gently over the surface creates a wonderfully calming and refreshing feature, especially on a hot day. By surrounding it with gravel topped with smaller boulders or beach pebbles a rock landscape is achieved. Adding a few other large rocks ensures this looks more like an erupting volcanic island set among a sea of pebbles.
DESIGN TIP *A feature like this can form part of a larger Japanese garden, but it would also make a pleasing water feature in another style of garden, to bring interest to an otherwise dull corner, perhaps where plants struggle to thrive.*

■ ABOVE
PATHWAYS Rocks with a suitably flat surface are sometimes used as stepping stones – through either lawn or water. They form a path that leads you through the garden, and the size and spacing of the stones are specially selected and positioned to dictate the pace at which you make the journey.
DESIGN TIP *Stepping stones placed close together slow up the speed of travel. Wider spacing will tend to speed up the pace. You can use different spacing to determine the rate at which the garden is to be explored, or vary the pace to meet the needs of different parts of the garden, perhaps dwelling on a feature of which you are specially proud.*

BUYING ROCK AND STONE

Garden centres and builders' merchants are likely to stock only a limited range or rocks and stones. Look in local directories for stone merchants – these should have a reasonable selection.

For a large feature it may be best to visit a suitable quarry, and perhaps select your rocks there. However, bear in mind that carriage is substantial on such a heavy material, so if possible use a local rock rather than one found perhaps in another part of the country, to save on carriage.

Know-how

SAND AND GRAVEL

Dry landscapes, with the emphasis on the element of stone, have their origins in the Zen style of gardening, its history originating from a form of Buddhism. This is a fascinating garden form to explore in specialist books on the subject, but you can imitate some of the elements in your own garden without an in-depth knowledge of the symbolism.

■ LEFT
GRAVEL OR SAND CIRCLES
Long straight lines of raked gravel or sand usually suggest calm water, and wavy lines evoke flowing water. Concentric circles in gravel also imply a sense of movement, perhaps where the water flows around an "island".
DESIGN TIP *To prevent gravel spilling over on to beds, borders, lawns or paths and ruining the design, it is important to have a firm, raised edge to a dry garden whenever possible.*

■ RIGHT
GRAVEL LINES
Where space is limited, a Japanese-style garden can be achieved by combining raked sand, rock and boulders and lantern in a vacant corner. The bridge here is for aesthetic purposes, rather than for practical reasons.
DESIGN TIP *Be cautious about using raked sand or gravel close to deciduous trees. Maintaining this neat appearance will be far from easy in autumn.*

■ ABOVE
COMPLEMENTING GRAVEL
The area of raked gravel or sand is usually limited, and here the path in the foreground is created from flat rounded stones, toning in with the almost mountain scree landscape of the rocks beside it.

DESIGN TIP *Be cautious about raked gravel where it might be used as a path or short-cut – it only takes one pair of feet to ruin the effect! Here a paved area has been provided around the edge to avoid this risk and provide a pleasing contrast.*

■ RIGHT
DRY BRIDGES Bridges can be built over dry garden "rivers" and "cascades", but these may spoil the scale of the landscape unless used with care.

DESIGN TIP *Dry gardens are striking features, but they can look a little barren to Western eyes. Plenty of plants in the background will help.*

Planning and Planting

A HINT OF THE ORIENT

A garden created totally in authentic Japanese style may not be appropriate for Western gardens, especially where the surrounding environment makes it seem alien. Some of the designs that follow on later pages show the Japanese influence more strongly, but this is one for anyone looking for a compromise with a strong Western influence.

PLANNING

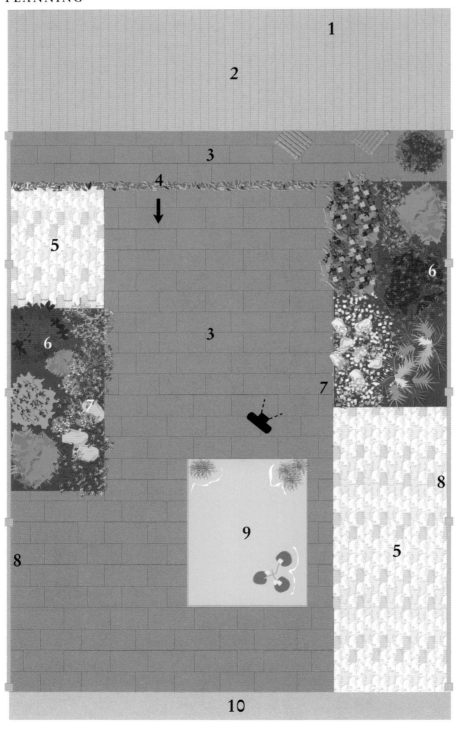

KEY TO PLAN

1   Bamboo screen
2   Covered patio in style of Japanese tea house
3   Paving slabs
4   Step
5   Granite setts
6   Specimen shrubs and herbaceous plants
7   Rocks and moss-covered pebbles
8   Stockade fence
9   Pond
10 House

↓ Direction of steps down
  Viewpoint on photograph

This garden is an ideal compromise between a family recreational area and a Japanese-influenced garden. Gardens often have to be a compromise between the conflicting requirements of different family members. Try to visualize what the garden will look like in winter. The use of a few choice evergreen shrubs and trees like rhododendrons and acers will ensure vital shape and form maintained throughout the year.

USING GRASSES

Grasses and small bamboos look effective in gravel or stone areas of borders. There are many varieties with interesting shapes and colours. Try planting contrasting groups for extra impact.

PLANTING

HOW TO PLANT GRASSES

1 Water the plants well and then knock them out of the pot and plant in well-prepared weed-free soil. If there are a lot of roots tightly wound around the edge of the pot, gently tease out some of them to encourage growth.

2 Some grasses are fast growers, so check first. If using a rampant grass, plant it in a large pot to restrict its spread. Dig a hole large enough to take the container, which must have drainage holes in it.

3 For spreading grasses, partly fill the container with soil then plant normally, with the rootball at the correct level. Firm the plant well, with your hand or heel, and add more soil if necessary.

4 Make sure the rim is flush with the surrounding soil (not below it, otherwise the grasses with creeping roots may escape). Water well, and keep well-watered until the plants are established.

Planning and Planting
STONE AND WATER

Two elements of symbolic importance in Japanese gardens are stone and water, both of which feature strongly in this design. This is a garden for contemplation and quiet admiration – not a family garden for children to play in. It's important to have a clear idea of what you want from this style, and to modify the degree of authenticity to suit.

PLANNING

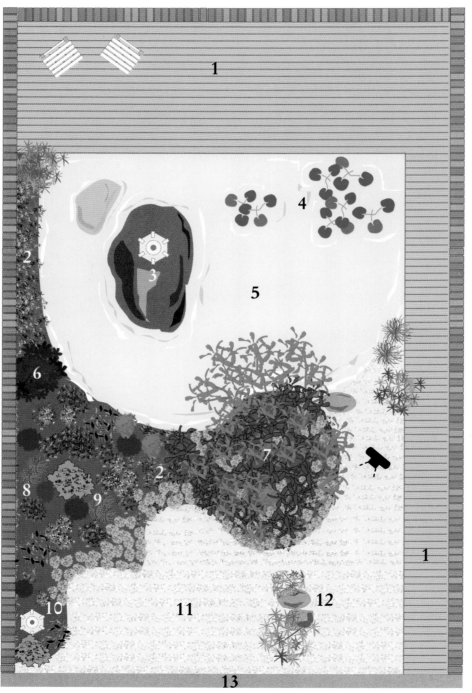

KEY TO PLAN

1 Timber decking
2 Mat-forming ground cover
3 Rock island with lantern
4 Water lilies
5 Pond
6 Specimen shrub
7 Specimen tree
8 Climber on wall
9 Dwarf shrubs
10 Japanese lantern
11 Raked gravel
12 Rocks and bamboo
13 House

◄ Viewpoint on photograph

This stylish Japanese garden makes extensive use of raked gravel, with rock "islands" and associated plants. In our plan, extensive use has also been made of water, another very pleasing visual and aural element that features strongly in the Japanese style of gardening. Plants have been used to create shapes and textures, and foliage effect is more important than colourful flowers. Before setting to work on this kind of garden, it's worth spending time doing some in-depth reading on Japanese gardens and their symbolism.

Although raked gravel is a very visual device, and highly attractive, you should bear in mind that the family dog and local wildlife or

PLANTING

playful children will quickly make re-raking an urgent priority if you are to keep it looking good. In addition, the area will require regular clearing and raking during the autumn to remove fallen leaves.

UNDERSTANDING LANTERNS

Japanese lanterns make a fascinating study worth reading up on or sending for catalogues from specialist suppliers. Their form and function are steeped in ancient conventions and traditions. In the mean time, it might be helpful to understand some of the basic terms: the parts of the lantern, the variety of styles and how the lantern should be positioned in relation to the house, if you want to be precise.

■ RIGHT
Lanterns may not have all the six parts illustrated here. The base may also be described as legs, pedestal or earth ring; the pillar called the trunk or shaft; and the roof referred to as the umbrella.

POSITIONING LANTERNS

■ ABOVE
Although most Western gardeners simply position their lanterns where they look pleasing, they should be angled towards a point where the centreline meets the house, as shown in the illustration.

THE PARTS OF A LANTERN

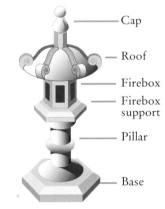

Cap
Roof
Firebox
Firebox support
Pillar
Base

KNOW YOUR STYLES

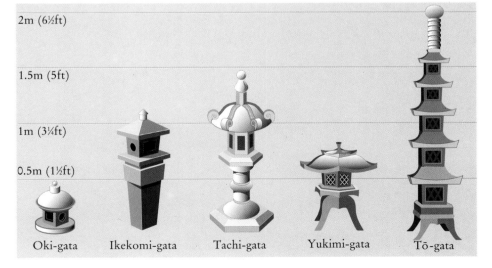

2m (6½ft)
1.5m (5ft)
1m (3¼ft)
0.5m (1½ft)

Oki-gata   Ikekomi-gata   Tachi-gata   Yukimi-gata   Tō-gata

Planning and Planting
A GARDEN OF ELEMENTS

Symbolism is important in a Japanese garden, and here rock, water and wood, all strong forces in nature, help to give this garden strong imagery.

PLANNING

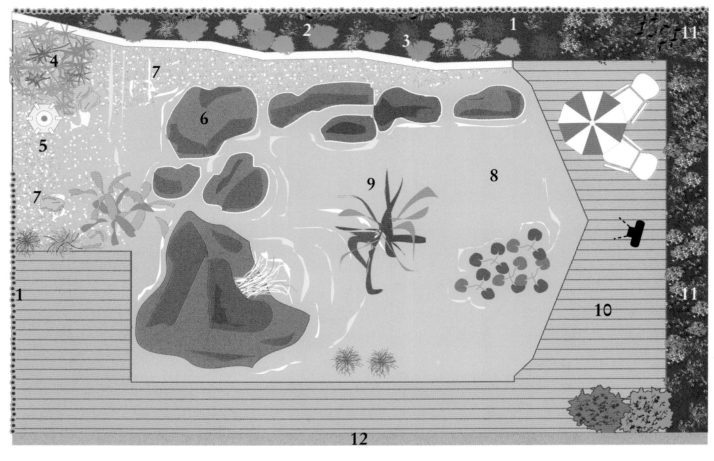

Because many features in Japanese gardens, such as water, rock and gravel mingled with plants, are designed to be viewed rather than sat among, it's important to provide suitable viewing areas. Decking blends in unobtrusively, and here it has been used on three sides to provide ample viewing angles as well as somewhere to sit and entertain.

A water feature like this, with a combination of rectangles and curves, and rocks placed within the pond, makes construction difficult for an amateur. It is worth taking professional advice when thinking about a creating a water feature of this size and complexity. Positioning heavy rocks also calls for teamwork.

DECIDING ON DECKING
Complicated decks with several changes in level or which project over water, for example, as here, require special construction techniques. There are companies who specialize in making and installing decking, and these should be consulted if you are in any doubt.

KEY TO PLAN

1 Bamboo screen
2 Climbers
3 Mound-forming plants
4 Bamboos
5 Japanese lantern
6 Rocks
7 Pebbles and gravel
8 Pond
9 Water irises
10 Timber decking
11 Dwarf shrubs
12 House

🔪 Viewpoint on photograph

PLANTING

HOW TO MAKE SIMPLE DECKING

1 Level the area to be decked, then position bricks or blocks on which the bearers will be supported. Bearers must be clear of the ground so that they are not in contact with damp earth and to allow air to circulate freely beneath the decking. If the ground is unstable, set the bricks or blocks on pads of concrete. Make sure they are level, or the final decking will not be stable.

2 Apply an additional coat of preservative to all fence posts. Lay out the posts provisionally, to check that the supports are spaced closely enough together and to ensure that they are cut so that two lengths butt over a support block. Lay heavy-duty polythene over the ground to prevent weeds growing though. Water will drain away where the sheets overlap.

3 Lay the posts over a waterproof membrane where they come into contact with the supporting bricks, and ensure that any joins are positioned over the support. Cut gravel boards to size and coat with preservative. Fix these to the posts using galvanized nails. Leave a gap of about 6mm (¼in) between each board to allow water to drain and the wood to swell safely.

Planning and Planting
SHADES OF GREY AND GREEN

Japanese-style gardens make their statements in a more subtle way than many of us are used to, often to stunning effect. Rocks like grey granite and grey gravel and pebbles have a bold yet restrained visual impact, and make a wonderful backdrop for the many shades of green foliage.

PLANNING

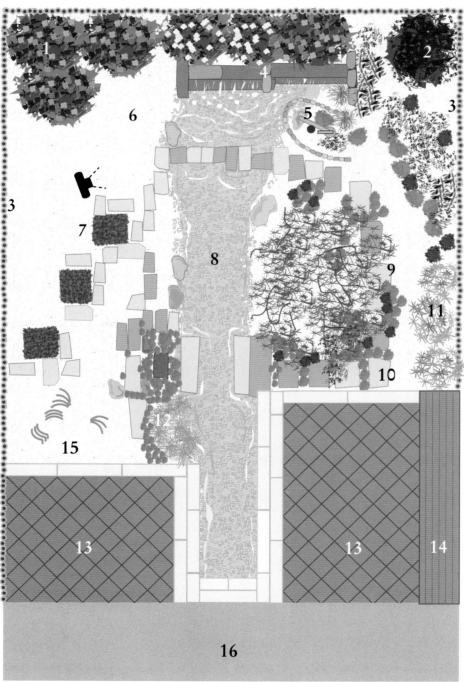

KEY TO PLAN

1 Rhododendron banks
2 Specimen tree
3 Bamboo fence
4 Granite retaining wall incorporating cascade
5 Deer scarer
6 Gravel
7 Clipped box squares
8 Stream with gravel bed
9 Pine tree with ground cover beneath
10 Stepping stones set into gravel
11 Bamboos
12 Dwarf rushes
13 Patio
14 Tea house
15 Terracotta tiles vertically embedded into gravel
16 House

⬏—Viewpoint on photograph

Water and rock play their usual important roles in this design, with the "stream" that runs the length of the garden being the central feature and holding the garden together. It draws the eye inward rather than to the boundaries, and the uncluttered open space generates an impression of size in a limited space. These are qualities that make the Japanese style suitable for gardens of all sizes, even small ones.

For a design like this to work properly, it's important to use appropriate materials. It is advisable to have a complex and possibly expensive garden like this constructed professionally, or at least take the advice of specialist suppliers before you start.

PLANTING

■ RIGHT

EASY-TO-MAKE TEA HOUSE This professional-looking tea house was made by an amateur from inexpensive and scrap wood, and shows what can be achieved with a little imagination and enthusiasm.

The side panels were made from a sheet of white material secured behind a home-made trellis constructed from battens, and the other walls were constructed from scrap timber. To make it visually acceptable and light on the inside, rolls of tied reeds were secured in position. The roof "tiles" are easy to make from feather-edged fencing boards, and the flashing around the finial at the top makes it weatherproof. As the wind can swirl into the open front, it is important with this kind of structure to secure the upright posts well into the ground. The seat was made from old railway sleepers (railroad ties), supported on short off-cuts of the same material. A black wood preservative on the exterior timber ensures this home-made structure has a really professional and authentic finish. Although the detailed construction of this kind of feature depends on the materials available, it shows what an excellent project a tea house makes for a do-it-yourself enthusiast.

Planning and Planting
MERGING WITH NATURE

Japanese gardens often reflect the natural world and its forces symbolically, but traditionally Japanese gardens are often designed to give a spectacular natural view from a vantage point, perhaps glimpsed as one bends down at a water basin. This garden simply becomes part of the landscape, natural and made-made merging almost imperceptibly. The large central pond is a striking central feature, but will need a regular care and maintenance to keep it looking its best.

PLANNING

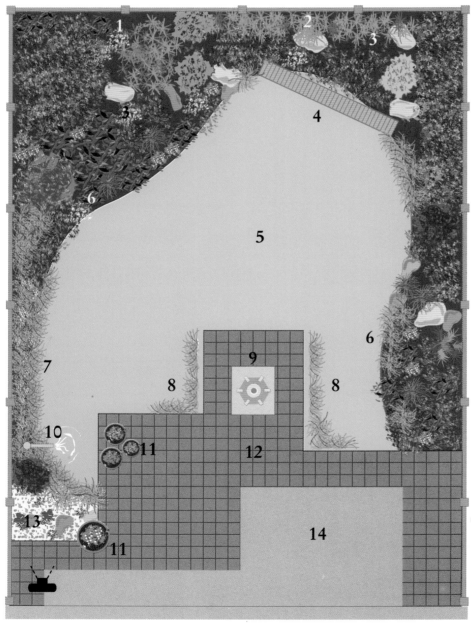

KEY TO PLAN

1   To open countryside
2   Bamboo hedge
3   Ornamental grasses and
    wild plants
4   Timber decking pontoon
5   Pond
6   Bog plants
7   Grasses and sedges
8   Marginal pond plants
9   Japanese lantern on pedestal
10 Bamboo water spout
11 Planted containers
12 Paving of granite setts
13 Gravel
14 House

⚘ Viewpoint on photograph

This garden almost merges with the landscape, but the mountains in the distance are in Switzerland, not Japan. Wherever there's a superb view, this kind of garden should appeal.

The whole garden revolves around the pond, the banks of which provide an opportunity for growing plenty of bog plants, blended with grasses and wild plants further back. This enables the garden to merge into the natural setting beyond, with no clear boundary when viewed from the house.

The more structured part of the garden, with its hard edges and rigid shapes, is confined to the area immediately outside the house. It is from this part of the garden that the view will be enjoyed, surrounded by the sights and sounds of nature. The bamboo spout adds to the musical sounds associated with water.

■ RIGHT

HOW TO MAKE A BAMBOO WATER SPOUT A water spout is quite easy to make. You may find it difficult to obtain lengths of bamboo of suitable thickness, but you can buy the spouts ready-made.

Buy a small plastic or glass-fibre reservoir, and sink this into the ground, a little below surface level. Place a small low-voltage pump in the reservoir, standing it on a brick to reduce the risk of the filter clogging with debris. Cover with a piece of strong metal mesh, larger than the reservoir.

Fix a length of flexible hose to the outlet of the pump, long enough to feed through the bamboo. Hollow out the bamboo if necessary, and cut a hole in the upright piece large enough to take the spout as a tight fit. Secure with a waterproof adhesive, then bind and tie black twine around the joint. Thread the hose through the spout and down the main stem, making sure it does not show. Then secure the bottom of the hose to the pump with a Jubilee clip.

Fill the reservoir, then test. It may be necessary to adjust the flow with a valve fitted to the pump – a gentle trickle is often more effective than a torrent. Make sure the water is not thrown beyond the reservoir. If it is, reduce the flow or lay pond liner around the area with the edge covered to channel the water back into the tank.

Cover the strong metal mesh with large pebbles completely. Heap up pebbles around the base of the bamboo to keep it stable.

As water will be lost through evaporation and splashes blown in the wind, check the reservoir periodically. The level must always cover the pump. Use a dipstick to tell you when it requires topping up without having to remove all the pebbles.

WATER PUMP

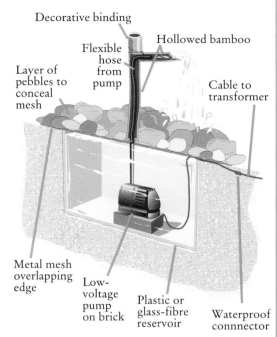

Decorative binding

Hollowed bamboo

Flexible hose from pump

Layer of pebbles to conceal mesh

Cable to transformer

Metal mesh overlapping edge

Low-voltage pump on brick

Plastic or glass-fibre reservoir

Waterproof connnector

PLANTING

Planning and Planting
FORCES OF NATURE

Not all oriental gardens are gentle and tranquil. Some use rocks and the forces of water in a more dramatic way. This garden uses the drama of rock banks and forceful cascades, as you might find on a wild mountainside.

PLANNING

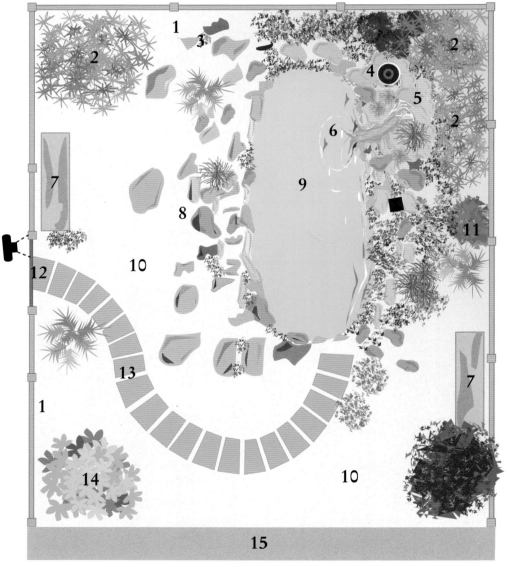

KEY TO PLAN

1 Decorative trellis
2 Clump of bamboo
3 Shrubs and Japanese acers
4 Japanese lantern
5 Rock bank
6 Cascade
7 Stone bench
8 Rocks and pebbles in gravel
9 Pond
10 Gravel
11 Shrubs
12 Gateway to side garden
13 Slab path set in gravel
14 Japanese acer
15 House

Viewpoint on photograph

To introduce a sense of calm to the rest of the garden, a large area of gravel has been used, together with restrained planting with bamboos and Japanese acers in key focal points.

ALONG THE GARDEN PATH

Paths in Japanese gardens tend to meander rather than lead in straight lines by the shortest route. Stepping stones are popular, as they affect the pace at which you proceed through the garden, as well as adding so much more character than ordinary paving slabs. These are a few ideas for stepping-stone paths.

When choosing stepping stones, an irregular shape is often more appealing than rectangular slabs of stone, but in the interests of safety try to ensure the actual stepping surface is reasonably flat and even.

Rock features like the one shown here are difficult and expensive to construct, and professional assistance will probably be required, but the effect is stunning by day and enchanting at night if the cascades are illuminated. A pond as large as this will also suit fish such as koi, which bring their own fascinating charm as they come up to feed. They also emphasize the Japanese theme.

PLANTING

STEPPING-STONE PATHS

■ ABOVE
Reasonably flat and evenly spaced stones make this an easy path to traverse, but these stones and the curve form an essential part of the design of the garden, and are much more interesting than a strictly functional garden path.

■ ABOVE
These stones project high above the surrounding ground and are irregularly spaced. Exploring this path, which is heavily planted on each side, is a more adventurous experience. It suggests a journey down a river full of obstacles, with dark and mysterious banks.

■ ABOVE
These stepping stones lead enticingly through a border of small shrubs, crossing a ribbon of pebbles that suggest a dried-up river bed. This use of paths makes even a short and simple journey to the bottom of the garden an exciting experience.

Choosing Plants

PLANTS FOR JAPANESE GARDENS

Make your Japanese garden more authentic by using mainly plants that originate in Japan. This is a part of the world that has given us many beautiful plants, and those illustrated below are only a tiny fraction of the wonderful plants available.

GRASSES AND BAMBOOS

Many bamboos are native to Japan and China, but some of them will grow too tall for a small garden. Where space is very limited, try the gold variegated *Pleioblastus auricomus* (*Pleioblastus viridistriatus* or *Arundinaria viridistriata*). Among the grasses native to Japan are several varieties of *Miscanthus sinensis*.

Pleioblastus auricomus is a plant of great beauty. It may also be found under its two synonyms *Pleioblastus viridistriatus* or *Arundinaria viridistriatus*. This gold and green variegated bamboo is compact and slow-growing.

JAPANESE MAPLES

Numerous acers are associated with Japan, but especially *Acer palmatum* and *A. japonicum*. There are many fine varieties of both species. *A. palmatum* makes a smaller tree, so it is a better choice.

There are many varieties of *Acer palmatum;* they all provide an effective display throughout the year and can be relied upon for some truly magnificent autumn colour.

CONIFERS

Among the conifers associated with Japan are some splendid varieties such as *Pinus densiflora*, *P. parviflora* and junipers such as *Juniperus chinensis*.

Pines come in many shapes and sizes, so be sure to choose an appropriate one for your Japanese garden. This is *Pinus densiflora* 'Jane Kluis'.

RHODODENDRONS AND CAMELLIAS

Many rhododendrons (including azaleas) and camellias are native to Japan, or have been bred there. There are large numbers of excellent varieties available. Both plants require an acid soil.

Rhodendrons and azaleas (which are types of rhododendron) are very popular Japanese shrubs, and readily available in garden centres, but they must have an acid soil to grow well. This one is an azalea called 'Ima-shojo' also known as 'Christmas Cheer'.

GROUND COVER

Ground-cover plants are used extensively in Japanese gardens, but of those grown mainly for foliage rather than for flowers, *Pachysandra terminalis* is typical, and it makes a green carpet about 30cm (1ft) high. There is also a variegated form. The grass-like, black-leaved *Ophiopogon planiscapus* 'Nigrescens' is often found in Japanese gardens.

Mosses feature as a ground cover in many genuine Japanese gardens, but these are difficult to cultivate to order in some climates, and not easily bought. *Sagina subulata*, still widely found under its older name of *S. glabra*, is a ground-hugging plant that resembles moss from a distance. There is a golden form called 'Aurea'. It will tolerate some frost but is not hardy in cold areas.

Ophiopogon planiscapus 'Nigrescens' is very distinctive with almost black grass-like foliage. It needs careful positioning in a light area of the garden otherwise it can be lost against a dark background. Use individual plants in juxtaposition with green foliage plants or flowering shrubs or plant it in a bold drift.

HOSTAS

These universally popular plants are widely grown in Japan, and some species are native to that country. There are dozens of readily available species and hybrids that would make excellent herbaceous plants for a Japanese garden, and they look good reflected in water.

Hostas are widely grown in Japan, and they are available in a wide range of leaf forms, many atractively variegated. They are a magnet for slugs; protect frequently.

JAPANESE IRIS

The iris most associated with Japanese water and bog gardens is *Iris ensata*. There are numerous varieties, all of which are attractive with big blooms that resemble a large-flowered clematis.

The Japanese iris is now called *Iris ensata*, but you may still find it sold as *I. kaempferi*. This attractive and popular variety is 'Mandarin'.

CLIMBERS

If you need to use a climber, choose one associated with Japan. The flowering climber *Wisteria floribunda*, sometimes called Japanese wisteria, is surely one of the most magnificent.

For foliage effect, try *Vitis coignetiae*, which has very large leaves with wonderful autumn colour. It looks especially pleasing growing over a bridge, but can be grown very successfully over a large pergola.

Only suitable for a large wall, but magnificent when its leaves turn crimson and scarlet before they fall, is the self-clinging *Parthenocissus tricuspidata*.

For something more unusual, try *Trachelospermum asiaticum*, an evergreen with creamy-white fragrant flowers, positioned against a warm, sunny wall.

Vitis coignetiae is a climber grown for its large leaves, which are especially beautiful in autumn when they turn crimson and scarlet. It is vigorous and can be grown through a tree, but can be confined by pruning if necessary.

ROCK AND WATER

Water has an almost magical attraction, holding a fascination for children and adults alike. Youngsters who show no interest in other garden construction jobs almost invariably become interested once a water feature is involved – a fact that may deter families with very young children. But water does not have to be deep and potentially dangerous: a flow just a fingertip deep along a rill can look cool and refreshing, and a pebble fountain will provide movement and sound with hazards reduced to a minimum. Wall fountains, especially self-contained ones where water flows into a shallow dish that forms part of the feature to be recirculated, make a wonderful focal point and are safe if small children are around.

Rock gardens, which are often combined with a pond, make interesting features in their own right and allow a large number of alpine plants to be grown in a relatively small area. Rock features work best on a naturally sloping site, but they can often be combined effectively with a pond or water course. The soil excavated from the pond can be used to form a raised bank, but be sure to cover any subsoil with prepared topsoil, otherwise the plants will languish.

■ ABOVE
A simple container full of pebbles can make a striking focal point.

■ OPPOSITE
Full of lush tranquillity, this city garden has only a small pond with little space
for true water plants, but use has been made of border plants such as hostas
and *Iris sibirica*, and the striking water hawthorn (*Aponogeton distachyos*).

INSPIRATIONAL IDEAS

Ponds and "streams" can form the centrepiece of your design. These will attract an amazing diversity of wildlife, and of course can be stocked with fish – which will become very tame if fed regularly during summer months.

■ ABOVE

A raised formal rectangular pond can be constructed from bricks or building blocks, rendered inside and out. It can be waterproofed using special resins or bitumen products obtainable from a pond supplier. The render on the outside can be painted a light colour to create a more attractive feature. Raised ponds are particularly useful for anyone who is disabled or infirm, or who finds bending difficult, as they bring the underwater wonders that much closer to eye level.

■ ABOVE

Imagine this scene as an ordinary lawn with just the borders at each side: pleasant but a trifle boring and without a strong sense of design. A simple pond in isolation would have been equally unappealing because there would be no sense of setting or height, and in winter it could look bleak and uninviting. Setting the pond in a larger circular area, however, with crescents of borders, paths and pebble areas, has given this section of the garden a sense of cohesion and design. The pebbles cleverly merge border and pond, and the sloping beach that drops away into the pond provides easy access for wildlife.

■ LEFT

In this water feature, the water flows directly into a submerged reservoir beneath a strong grille that supports the stone and boulders, making it safe for even small children. Occasionally, genuine millstones are used for this kind of feature, but these are extremely heavy to handle and support, as well as being expensive and difficult to obtain. Fortunately, convincing glass-fibre imitations that look just as good, and which are much easier to handle and install, are available. You can buy them as part of a kit that includes the reservoir, and all you have to provide are the boulders or pebbles.

Although these kinds of feature can be set among plants, they tend to look most effective in a courtyard or dry-looking area as shown here.

INSPIRATIONAL IDEAS

Rock and water features are perfect tools for gardeners fond of strong, bold statements of shape and form. They also offer the opportunity for growing a range of colourful water and bog plants.

■ **BELOW**
Making use of the strong textures of water and slate, this Japanese-style garden is a study in shape and form. Although this kind of water feature may not appeal to a plant-lover – the only water plants apart from a water lily are water hyacinths (*Eichhornia crassipes*), both of which will die down in winter – it will appeal to someone whose sense of design is stronger than their love of plants and bright flowers.

■ LEFT
Formal ponds can be pleasing but water can also be used in a natural way. The shape and dense planting around the edge of this pond create the illusion that it is a natural part of the landscape. Although close to the boundary fence, taking the pond beneath a bridge gives the illusion of water flowing far beyond. Bridges themselves are almost always focal points, and they usually entice visitors to walk over them to explore the garden on the other side. A pond or "stream" provides the justification for building a bridge.

■ RIGHT
A pond may not always be appropriate, but a small running-water feature like this one can have just as much impact. In this design, the circular basins reflect the curves in other parts of the garden, and although it would have made a pleasing feature anywhere, its impact is that much stronger because it clearly looks part of an overall design.

Know-how

FORMAL PERFECTION

Water features can easily be added to an existing garden, but they will look more integrated if you plan for them early on in the design process. Rock gardens are more difficult to add at a late stage without their looking like a very artificial mound of earth, and they almost always work best when landscaped into the basic garden plan.

If you want fish and flowers in your pond, choose an open site that will receive sun for at least half the day if possible, and is away from overhanging deciduous trees unless you are prepared to net the pond and clear the leaves from the water to prevent pollution. The majority of rock plants also require a sunny position.

Formal ponds, with their regular outlines and geometric shapes, look best in gardens designed to a rigid grid where the same lines are carried through to other parts of the garden. They offer less scope for pondside planting and associated bog areas than informal ponds do, but provide plenty of scope for aquatic plants and fish.

■ **BELOW**
BREAKING UP PAVING Although this pond is relatively small, it makes an impact because it forms a focal point in a strongly geometric design. Water can be a vital element in counteracting the potential harshness of a large amount of paving. The wall mask ensures the area will remain attractive even when the pond plants have died back.
DESIGN TIP *To avoid an expanse of paving appearing monotonous, use materials of a contrasting colour to pick out a design or to emphasize a change of level. Here, bricks and terracotta tiles have been used to provide contrast and to add a touch of colour to a large area of paving.*

■ **LEFT**
LONG AND FORMAL Formality is the essence of this style of garden, and water is the central feature around which the garden has been designed. It is essentially a garden for a warm climate, or at least where the illusion of a warm-climate garden is required, but a variation on this style of gardening could make a stunning town garden.
DESIGN TIP *Where water is a major feature, always consider how the garden will look in winter. Pumps will have to be turned off in very cold climates, and a pond's frozen surface can look bleak. To compensate, include plenty of evergreens and make lavish use of decorative pots and ornaments around the water feature.*

■ BELOW

UNUSUAL SHAPES Formal ponds are practical for even a
small front garden, and the strong design and impressive
planting in this one ensure it will be pleasing all the year round.
The introduction of a stepping platform to connect the two
ponds ensures they link the garden rather than divide it.
DESIGN TIP *If the visual aspects of gravel appeal but you are
worried about the loose stones being kicked around on a path that
is used frequently, consider bonded gravel, which has been used on
these paths. The small stones are bonded to a resin instead of being
laid loose. The effect is equally as attractive as loose gravel.*

■ ABOVE

CASCADES A garden created on a gentle slope provides
scope for cascades and tumbling water, and in this garden the
formal water chute and rectangular pond reflect the overall
design, with its straight lines and right angles.
DESIGN TIP *Allow the overall design of the garden to dictate the
style of pond you create. In this garden, with its dominant straight
lines, an informal wildlife pond with meandering outline and
shallow beaches around the edge would have looked incongruous.*

RECTANGULAR PONDS

Rectangular ponds can be
constructed with a liner, but
this involves pleating it at the
corners, which can look
unattractive unless masked by
careful planting. It is possible
to have box-welded liners made
by specialist suppliers,
otherwise render a concrete or
building-block pond and
waterproof it with a resin or
bitumen-based product
manufactured for the purpose.

Know-how

NATURAL INFORMALITY

Informal ponds are usually easier to construct than formal ones and are preferred by wildlife because access to the water is usually easier and the surrounding planting provides useful shelter. Informal ponds also provide an excuse to introduce a bog garden.

■ LEFT
NATURAL POND
This garden is completely informal, yet it has a strong sense of design and structure, which the bridge and trellis help to emphasize. The irregular informal shape and rocks give the illusion of a natural pond, and the lush planting helps to mask neighbouring gardens.
DESIGN TIP *An informal pond can be used to encourage a sense of exploration and may make your garden seem larger than it really is. Having access around all sides, or a bridge linking paths, will appear intriguing.*

■ RIGHT
PEBBLES This kind of natural-looking water course can be created easily with a liner, the edge of which can be well hidden by beach pebbles. With this kind of covering, a drop in water level though evaporation will not be noticeable as there is no obvious water line. It must flow into a deep area at the end, however, so that the submerged pump remains covered.
DESIGN TIP *Don't think only in terms of fish ponds when introducing water. Features like this one can be even more effective if you want to create the illusion of a wild or natural garden. They will still attract lots of wildlife which will come to the garden to drink and bathe.*

CLEAR WATER

Even the most well-designed pond will be unattractive if the water is green. Most ponds turn green for a few days or weeks each year, usually in spring and early summer when the water is warming up, but the aquatic plants are not sufficiently grown to reduce the amount of sunlight reaching the water. A pond that remains green for long periods requires treatment.

Green water is caused by millions of free-floating algae, which feed on nutrients in the water, multiplying rapidly in warm, sunlit water. Avoid adding nutrient-rich soil to the pond, and do not use ordinary fertilizer on pond plants.

There are chemical controls of various kinds, but they vary in effectiveness, their effect can be short-lived, and the dead algae can cause problems with falling oxygen levels as they decay (which may kill fish). The most satisfactory way to deal with green water is to install a UV (ultra-violet) clarifier. This will require a power supply for the special lamp and a pump to circulate the water. Provided you choose a unit powerful enough for the capacity of your pond (consult your supplier), the water should begin to clear within days.

■ ABOVE

STREAM-FED POND Regular clearing and planting with a range of water lilies and other plants has transformed this natural stream-fed pond into a wonderful garden feature. The banks have been planted for year-round interest, and ornaments provide useful focal points in winter when most of the vegetation has died down.

DESIGN TIP *Don't forget to incorporate a few garden seats, even in an informal garden. You will get more out of your garden if there's somewhere to sit and relax. Here, the addition of a couple of colourful cushions has transformed an ordinary garden bench into a comfortable focal point from which to view your garden.*

■ RIGHT

CLOSE TO THE HOUSE This pond has been taken up to the conservatory, then a deck has been built out over the water. Pondlife, especially the fish, can be enjoyed from the deck on a sunny day and from the conservatory when the weather is less inviting.

DESIGN TIP *Use plants to create privacy and a sense of seclusion. Here the dense planting masks a busy road.*

Know-how

MOVING WATER

Still water brings calm and tranquillity to a garden, but sometimes a sense of vibrancy and life is needed. A tumbling "stream" introduces an authentic feeling of the wild to a garden, but sound and movement can be created with equal effect by a tinkling fountain, a tumbling cascade or a simple water spout fixed to a wall. Whichever you choose, moving water is almost certain to become one of the garden's most exciting focal points.

■ RIGHT
WATER STAIRS
Although an
ambitious project,
a flight of water
stairs can be
attention-grabbing
as well as musical.
Building them on
a curve makes the
most of the limited
space available, and
in this case the
feature makes a
splendid centrepiece
for the garden.
DESIGN TIP
*Don't be put off by
an ambitious project
simply because you
lack construction
skills. Hire a
contractor to do the
building to your own
specific designs.*

THINK ABOUT FLOW

Whether installing a cascade or
a fountain, it's important to
choose a pump with an
appropriate flow rate (which is
measured in gallons or litres an
hour). This is a complex area as
it also depends on whether the
same pump has to share the
operation of a biological filter,
or perhaps another cascade or
fountain. Go to a reputable
water garden specialist for
advice. Some will even allow
you to exchange the pump if it
does not do the job.

Large flows will require a
high-voltage pump, but most
small fountains operate
satisfactorily from a low-
voltage pump.

■ LEFT
SMALL FOUNTAIN Without moving water, even well-
designed small patio ponds may lack impact. A fountain will
add to the formal atmosphere, and in a small garden the sound
will not be as potentially overpowering as that from a cascade.
DESIGN TIP *Corners can be difficult areas to fill creatively, but
a corner pond with an attractive fountain will make excellent use
of otherwise wasted space.*

■ OPPOSITE
MOORLAND STREAM It takes years
of experience and a lot of effort to
construct a moorland stream to this
standard, including a knowledge of the
natural landscape and the mechanics and
flow rates of pumps, but a more modest
version is within the scope of an
enthusiastic amateur.
DESIGN TIP *Unless your garden is on a
natural slope, keep the fall from top to
bottom of the "stream" relatively modest.
This will avoid too much earth-moving
and reduce the need to manhandle heavy
rocks, yet the effect can be just as stunning
as cascades with large falls.*

■ RIGHT
WALL FOUNTAIN A wall fountain
can transform any backyard or courtyard
wall. A trickling spout of water will add
to the visual and auditory pleasures of
the garden. This one is particularly
ornate, but in an area where there may
not be much else to arrest the attention,
being bold can bring rich rewards.
DESIGN TIP *Bear in mind that the
higher the position of the water spout
above the receptacle, the louder the sound
will be. In a confined area, a strong flow
from a height could become irritating for
you or your neighbours. Fortunately, most
pumps have a flow adjuster.*

Know-how

ON THE ROCKS

Rockwork can be difficult to work into a garden plan, and will be much easier on a sloping site than on a flat one. Don't think only of traditional rock garden banks, however, as rock outcrop beds can be equally pleasing and are much easier to construct in gardens without a natural slope.

PEAKS AND TROUGHS

Rock gardens are at their best in spring, and by comparison they can seem rather dull at other times of the year. Do not allow this commonly cited drawback to deter you from using rock features. By choosing plants that flower at different seasons, and including evergreens and winter-flowering bulbs for the bleakest months, a rock garden can be packed with interest every month of the year.

Try using annuals to fill in any gaps for the summer, even if they are not strictly alpines, but make sure they don't seed readily and thereby become a nuisance in future seasons.

■ ABOVE LEFT
ROCKERY BORDER An artificial mound in a flat garden does not always work as well as this example, especially if the mound is low and only small pieces of rock are used. This mound is substantial enough to make a positive feature, and it has plenty of evergreens and winter-flowering heathers to make it attractive the year round.
DESIGN TIP *To prevent a rockery from looking stark in winter, be sure to plant sufficient evergreens as well as alpines in this kind of rock garden.*

■ LEFT
SLOPING ROCK GARDEN A gentle slope like this makes an ideal natural-looking rock garden. A rock garden of this size will accommodate a large number of plants and is ideal for anyone who wants to specialize in alpines. A path through the rocks is perfect for viewing these small plants close up.
DESIGN TIP *The natural effect would have been spoilt if the steps had run up through the centre in a straight line. A staggered or meandering path is less obtrusive, and is likely to be less tiring to climb than one that goes straight up by the shortest route.*

■ ABOVE

ROCKY BANKS Rock and water make happy partners, and this weathered limestone is especially attractive. This garden is on the grand scale, but a smaller version could be constructed for a more modestly sized garden.

DESIGN TIP *Follow any natural contours in the ground wherever possible to minimize the amount of earth-moving required.*

■ LEFT

FEATURE ROCKERY This rock feature could be incorporated into most informal designs. It's simply a bed cut into the lawn, and even a small area like this can be densely planted. The rock is tufa, a soft, porous stone into which planting holes can be easily drilled if necessary.

DESIGN TIP *Keep the height of a rock bed in proportion to its size. A small bed should have only a low mound, a large bed can be higher. If you plant densely, as has been done in this rock feature, height is relatively unimportant.*

127

Planning and Planting

CHANGING LEVEL

Rock gardens are sometimes used as a design solution for a steep slope, where rock out-crops can look very convincing. If the slope is more gentle and the setting inappropriate for a large conventional rock garden, it may be possible to make the most of a raised rock bed. This one forms a natural break between a level upper lawn and a larger sloping lawn that leads to the rest of the garden.

1 Specimen tree
2 Hedge
3 Mixed border
4 Specimen shrubs
5 Outbuilding
6 Slope to lower lawn
7 Path
8 Rhododendrons
9 Lawn
10 Raised rock bed
11 To side garden
12 Patio of crazy
    paving

13 Crazy paving
14 Small specimen tree
15 Steps
16 Dwarf shrubs
17 Path around house
18 House
← Direction of steps
    and slope down
    Viewpoint on
    photograph
✕ Garden continues

PLANNING

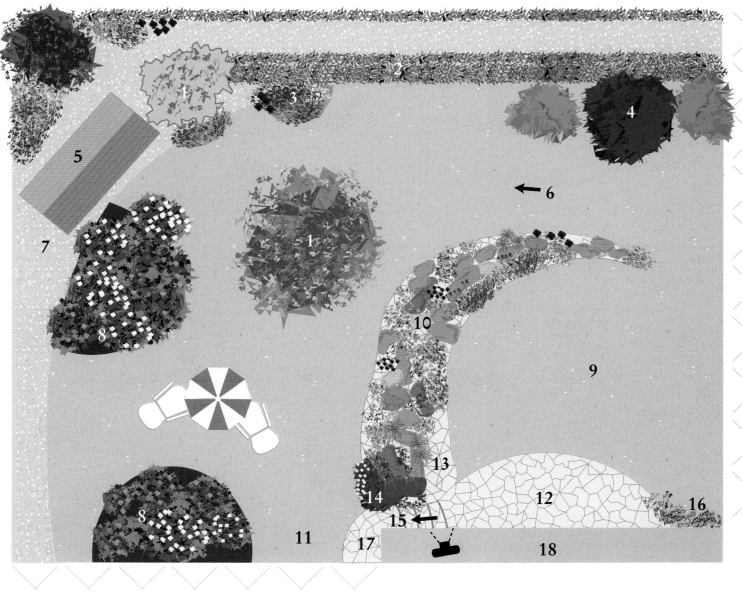

SLOPING GARDENS

Even gently sloping gardens pose the problem of how to integrate the various levels. Steep gardens are often terraced, although this is a labour-intensive and often expensive option. Where the height difference is small enough to make mowing a safe and practical routine, a gently sloping lawn is a sensible option. Here, a flat area of patio and lawn has been created at the front of the house, with the lawn falling away beyond the rock bed.

Rock beds make pleasing features, but they look best where they have a purpose. Here, the rock bed acts as a divider, with the ground falling away more on one side than the other.

MAKING A ROCK GARDEN

A raised rock bed like this one can be made on a level site if necessary, or you could build one at the back of a pond using the excavated soil for the basic mound. In either case good fertile soil should be used for the planting areas. Locally quarried rocks are usually cheaper and blend in with the area.

PLANTING

1 Build up soil to form a raised area of appropriate size. Always ensure there is a space between the soil and any fence or wall, and be careful not to bridge any damp-proof course in nearby brickwork.

2 Mix together equal parts of soil, coarse grit and peat and spread evenly over the mound. Lay the first rocks at the base, trying to keep the strata running in the same direction.

3 Position the next row of rocks. Use rollers and levers to move them. Ensure that the sides all slope inwards, and make the top reasonably flat rather than building it into a pinnacle.

4 Position the plants. As each layer is built up, add more of the soil mixture, and consolidate it around the rocks. Finish by covering the exposed soil with a thin layer of horticultural grit, to improve the appearance.

Planning and Planting
FOCUS ON CIRCLES

Circular themes are almost always distinctive, and they make striking gardens even with minimal planting. This kind of garden depends very much on structure for impact, and the focal point here is a fantastic water feature that uses both sight and sound to command attention.

PLANNING

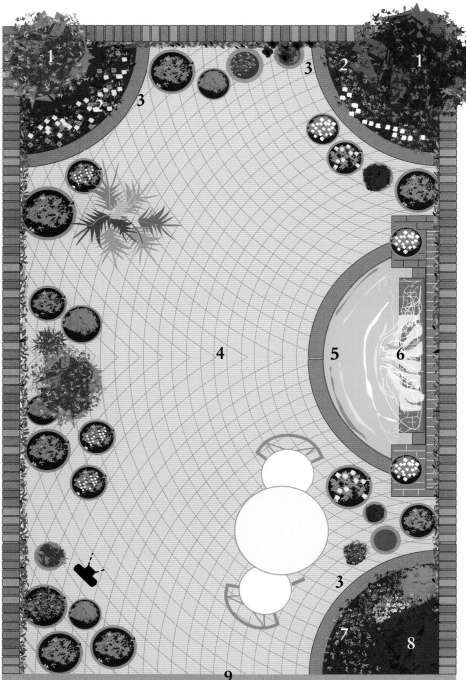

Circular themes can make use of full circles or crescents and arcs, sometimes overlapping as shown here. The three corner beds make use of quadrants. There's a sense of symmetry about this kind of garden, but simple mirror images could make it a little too predictable, and another cascade opposite this one would probably detract from the impact. The sound of two tumbling sheets of water might also cross the threshold between being pleasant and irritating.

Although there are plenty of pots in this design, little other maintenance is required so it is not especially labour-intensive. Pots of seasonal plants help to provide that vital dash of colour.

The choice of paving and the bricks used for the raised beds is also important in a garden like this. Here colours and textures have been chosen that blend together well, but if bricks and paving had been chosen with colours that did not harmonize, the overall effect might have been much less pleasing.

PLANTING

■ RIGHT
WALL MASKS AND SPOUTS
This kind of cascade is really a job for a
professional or very experienced
amateur, but it is possible to create a
water spout on a more modest scale.
A high wall isn't necessary, as a gentle
flow with a drop of 60–90cm (2–3ft)
may sound more musical than a torrent
from a high spout. Unless the feature is
large, a low-voltage pump should be
adequate, but choose one with a flow
adjuster so that you have more control.

Metal pipework can be used, but
plastic pipes are perfectly adequate.
The difficulty lies in concealing pipes.
Whenever possible, drill a hole through
the wall and run the pipework up the
back, bringing it back through the wall
at the appropriate height. Disguise any
unsightly pipes with an evergreen
climber, such as ivy.

CROSS-SECTION OF A WALL MASK OR SPOUT

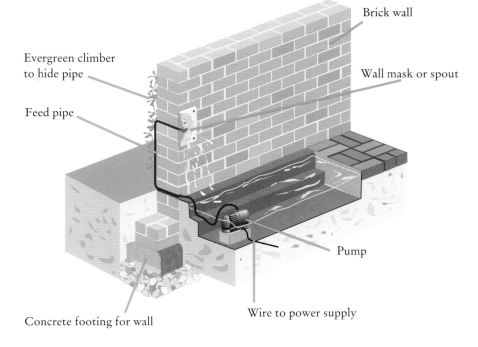

Brick wall

Evergreen climber
to hide pipe

Wall mask or spout

Feed pipe

Pump

Wire to power supply

Concrete footing for wall

Planning and Planting
CLASSIC ROMANCE

With a little imagination you can bring a dream garden with classic connotations to life, even in a small town garden. All you need are some materials from a company specializing in reclaimed demolition materials and a vivid imagination.

PLANNING

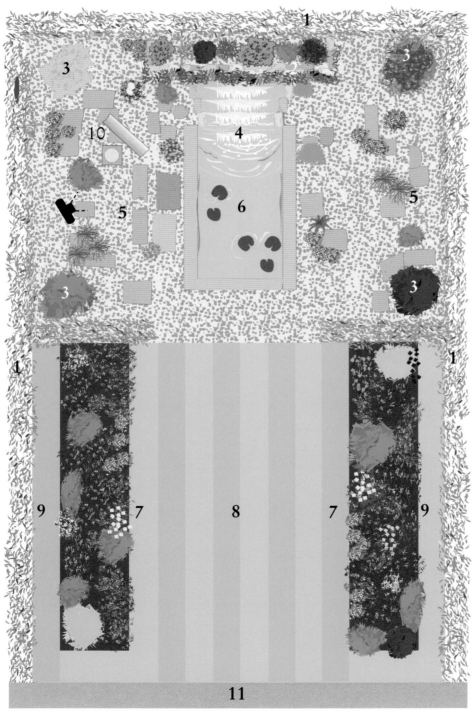

KEY TO PLAN

1 Yew hedge
2 Shrubs and climbers
3 Specimen shrub
4 "Staircase" cascade
5 Plants and paving set in gravel
6 Formal pond
7 Herbaceous border
8 Lawn
9 Grass access strip to rear of border
10 Reclaimed classical pillar and plinth
11 House
⬛ Viewpoint on photograph

This is a garden for the romantic with a love of traditional gardens and a classical style. The "staircase" cascade forms the focal point, and it sets the tone for this part of the garden. Because it has been constructed mainly from reclaimed building materials from old houses, it has a timeless quality that can transform a town garden into a romantic piece of the past. The clever use of an old pillar, positioned so that it looks as though it fell from its pedestal many years ago, creates a wonderful sense of atmosphere.

Good old-fashioned herbaceous borders flanking the lawn reflect a formal style of gardening once popular, and the traditional yew hedges hold the two parts of the garden together.

When using reclaimed materials, it's best to have a flexible approach. Be prepared to modify your plans according to the materials you can obtain.

PLANTING

■ BELOW
CONSTRUCTING WATER STAIRS
The actual method of construction will
depend on the materials used and the
size of the feature, but the same
principles can be applied to most forms
of water stairs.

After excavating the pond area, form a
consolidated slope of soil at an
appropriate angle, taking into account
the height of each step. On a natural
slope you may only have to cut into the
bank; on a flat site it will be necessary to
build it up and compact the ground.

Lay the pond liner first. Then lay a
sheet of liner along the slope, leaving
enough material to fold up at the sides
to ensure a watertight channel. Use a
liner underlay to protect it from stones,
and it is worth using an extra layer of
liner as access, for repairs will be
difficult once construction is finished.

Lay a concrete pad on the bottom of
the pond to support the brick wall. Place
a piece of spare liner over the bottom of
the pond, folded over a couple of times,
then construct a brick support wall to
the height of the first riser.

Bed the first step on mortar, ensuring
it has a slight slope forwards, but is level
from left to right. Lay each of the other
steps in the same way. At the top, make
a chamber a couple of bricks high into
which the return hose can be fed. Cover
this with another slab or stone.

Ensure the liner comes up to the level
of each step at the sides – it will be
necessary to trim it to size. Be careful
not to trim too short, and if possible
leave it long enough to tuck into the soil
mounded against each side. Plant
lavishly with evergreens to hide the
edges and any trace of the liner.

Once the mortar is completely dried,
connect the pump and check for any
leaks. A powerful pump will be required
to ensure a fast flow of water over the
edge of each lip. Consult an aquatic
specialist for advice about the flow
requirements before you buy. Also
check on hose sizes and fittings. If in
doubt, go for a larger size, as you can
always turn down the flow if necessary.

CROSS-SECTION OF WATER STAIRS

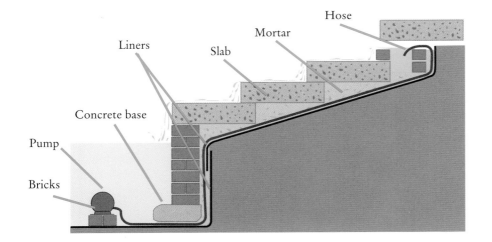

Planning and Planting
MODERN IMAGE

Instead of thinking of ponds and cascades when designing with water in mind, try visualizing water as a texture, rather like an area of paving or gravel. This garden shows how smart water can look in a modern setting. Don't be afraid to use water imaginatively: although the amount used in this garden is small, it's one of the most interesting and creative features in an already fascinating and exciting garden.

PLANNING

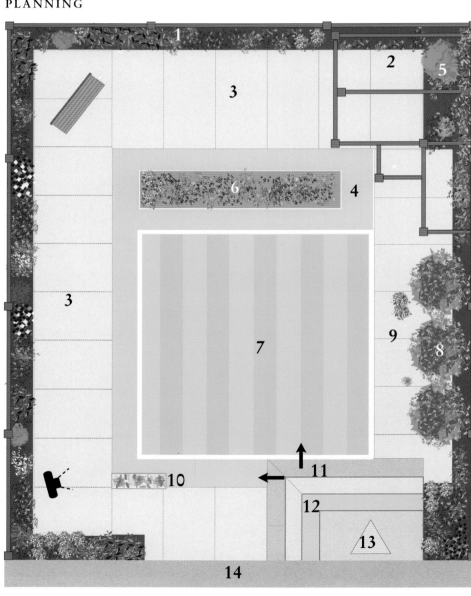

As this garden makes the most of shapes and textures, it is likely to appeal to someone who loves to explore design ideas rather than to a plant enthusiast. Apart from the lawn, which requires regular cutting, it's also very low-maintenance. The water-framed lawn is perhaps the main focal point, so it's essential that the grass is kept short and looking lush, and care must be taken not to allow grass clippings to fall into the watery surround.

Ordinary paving slabs could have been used for economy, but the choice of a natural stone such as slate gives it a more sophisticated appearance and a stronger sense of design. Where paving is a dominant feature in a garden, it is worth spending time and money to select the most suitable material.

Where natural stone forms an important part of the design, it is worth visiting a few stone merchants or quarries to discuss your requirements in detail. They may be able to advise and perhaps assist with the selection and cutting of the stone.

PLANTING

■ RIGHT

PERGOLA POSSIBILITIES Although rustic poles are often used for rose pergolas, in design terms a sawn timber (lumber) pergola is a better choice. It will also be able to support heavy climbers such as wisterias. Use preservative-treated wood (but avoid using creosote if planting soon after erection), and treat cut surfaces before assembling. Fix the uprights securely, setting them in concrete or securing them in post spikes, always using a spirit level to check verticals.

Assemble the overhead sections "dry" on the ground to make sure the joints all fit well, but don't nail them yet. Halving joints are suitable for the overhead beams, but the lower halves will have to be nailed to the uprights before the top halves are assembled.

The halving joints are best screwed together, but drill starter holes while the assembly is on the ground, as it will be difficult to drill at a height.

If the pergola is long, overhead beams will have to be joined, which should be done over a post. Use galvanized nails or zinc-plated screws.

FIXING A POST **HALVING JOINT** **JOINING BEAMS**

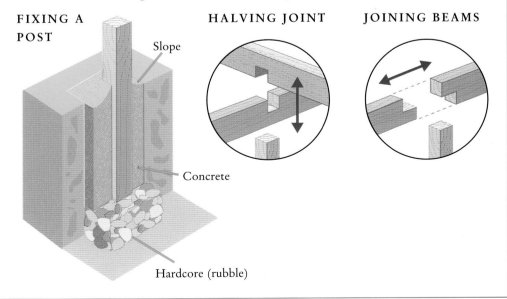

Slope

Concrete

Hardcore (rubble)

Planning and Planting
NATURAL SLOPE

Gardens with a gentle slope offer an ideal opportunity for constructing a natural-looking rock and water feature, with perhaps a stream and a small cascade. For ease of construction, these features may have to follow the natural contours of the site, and this may influence your design.

KEY TO PLAN

1	Garden bench	10	Dwarf conifer
2	Lawn	11	Patio
3	Rock garden	12	Plants in containers
4	Slope and step	13	House
5	Pond		
6	Cascade	↑	Direction of steps down
7	Stream		
8	Mixed border	◣	Viewpoint on photograph
9	Header pool		

A naturally sloping garden is ideal for a rock and water feature, but your design will be determined largely by the slope and profile of the ground. Where practical, choose a rock type found in your locality: it will look more natural, and it will almost certainly be cheaper than rock that has been transported over long distances.

Planting plans are difficult to devise for a rocky slope, so concentrate on a few key plants, such as dwarf conifers and dwarf evergreen shrubs. The smaller rock plants are usually best planted intuitively, choosing subjects that fit both the space available and the setting.

A meandering path is always more interesting than a straight one, and a combination of sloping path and a few steps changes the pace and makes the slope easier to cope with.

Seating also requires careful thought. It's worth providing a refuge large enough to take a seat part-way down to help those who find slopes difficult. Choosing a position that has an attractive view of the garden, or of the scene beyond, will encourage more use of the seat.

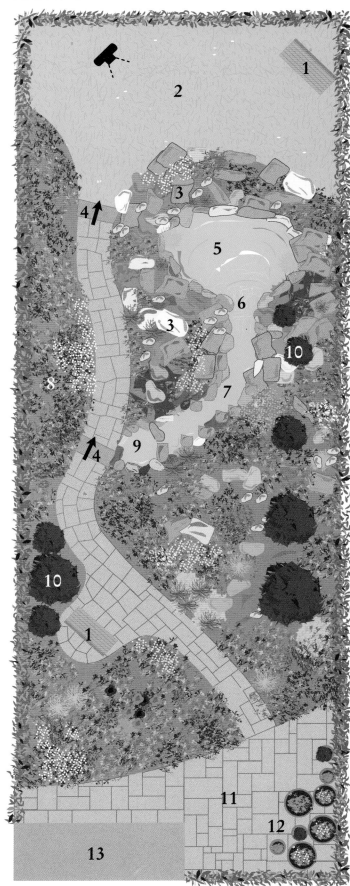

PLANTING

■ **RIGHT**
MAKING A ROCK STREAM
A stream can be constructed from a series of separate long, narrow ponds, with the liners overlapped and sealed where the levels change.

Use a good-quality liner over a proper liner underlay, and make small concrete slabs at each side of the level changes on which to bed suitable rocks. Fold over a piece of spare liner to form an extra cushion under the concrete pad.

The stream is made watertight at the cascades by overlapping the liner from the higher pond over that from the lower (see illustration opposite). This should prevent water escaping, but as an additional precaution seal the overlaps with special tape or adhesive. Consult your aquatic supplier regarding materials, as it depends on the type of liner used.

Bed the rocks firmly on each side of the cascade on mortar to ensure they are

stable. You may, however, first want to have a test run, then drain the water to make any adjustments. An aquatic specialist should be able to advise on a

suitable pump – it will need to be powerful to maintain a fast flow over a wide lip. A header pool is used at the top, fed by a return hose from the pump.

CROSS-SECTION OF A ROCK STREAM

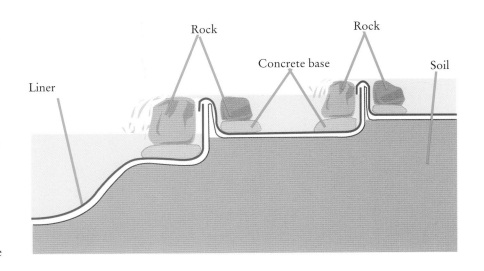

Planning and Planting
TRADITIONAL FORMALITY

Large gardens normally require large ponds to have any impact, but by creating a formal area to frame a small formal pond it's still possible to create a big impact.

Very large gardens are often difficult to design, especially if you want to introduce a formal style. Here the problems have been overcome by using an area near the house for a lawn, with a low clipped hedge to mark the boundary between the formal and informal areas. Within

PLANNING

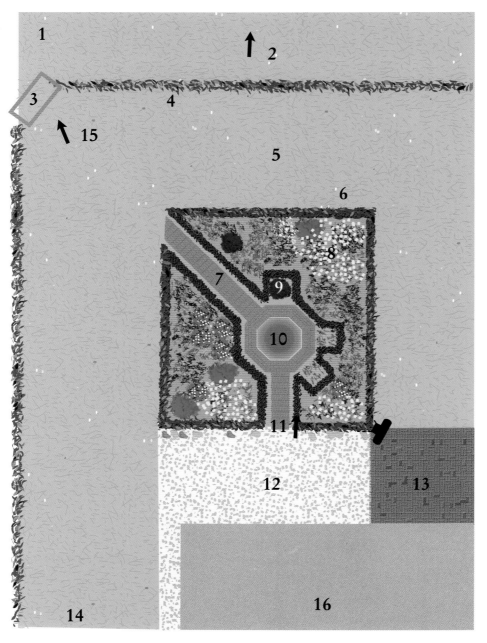

this formal part of the garden an enclosed mini-garden has been introduced with a central pond.

The disparate parts of the garden have been linked by the path layout within the enclosed formal garden. One of the main paths is aligned at right angles to the house so this is the feature you see as you leave the house. The other main path swings around the pool to leave in a direct line with the pergola in the corner of the lawn.

AN ALPINE WHEEL
If you have small children, you may prefer an alternative to the central circular pond in this design. Instead, you could build a fragrant herb wheel or a pretty alpine wheel. You will need: two lengths of wood, string, spade, garden compost and fertilizer, an old drain cover, bricks, fine gravel, pebbles and slates for decoration, and of course a selection of alpines.

MAKING AN ALPINE WHEEL

1 Dig over the soil and enrich with fertilizer and garden compost. Tie a piece of wood at each end of a piece of string the length of the radius. While someone holds the central peg, scribe the circle while keeping the string taut. Lay bricks around the circumference and to form the spokes of the wheel.

2 Position the plants on the wheel while still in their pots, to check the spacing, then plant. Plant each section of the wheel with a different variety so that, as they grow, they will help to define the design. A contrast of colours and textures of leaves will look most effective.

3 Cover the surface of exposed soil with gravel, then add decorative pebbles and slates to improve the appearance while the plants grow to their full potential.

Choosing Plants
WATER AND ROCK PLANTS

Choosing water and rock plants can be bewildering: there are always more desirable plants to grow than there's space for. For a balanced pond, it's important to choose some submerged oxygenators even though they have little visual appeal, as well as deep-water plants such as water lilies to provide vital foliage cover over part of the surface. However, it's among the marginal plants (those planted in shallow water at the edge) and bog plants for wet ground outside the pond that the greatest variety can be found.

WATER LILIES
It's important to select suitable varieties. Some of the most vigorous ones are suitable only for lakes and very large ponds, while others are miniatures suitable for water features in sinks and tubs. If in doubt, always check with your supplier. Good ones for a small pond are 'Froebeli' (red) and 'Rose Arey' (pink). For medium-sized ponds, suitable varieties include 'Amabilis' (pink), 'Attraction', 'Laydeckeri Purpurata' (red) and 'Marliacea Chromatella' (yellow).

Nymphaea 'Amabilis' is one of many beautiful water lilies suitable for a medium-sized pond. Although water lilies are relatively expensive to buy, they will provide years of pleasure.

OTHER PLANTS FOR DEEP WATER
So-called deep-water plants are grown with about 30cm (1ft) or more of water above their crowns, although most will grow in water more than twice this depth. Water lilies are the best-known deep-water aquatics, but try the water hawthorn (*Aponogeton distachyos*), which has slightly fragrant white flowers that bloom from spring to autumn. It can be rampant if planted directly in mud at the bottom of the pond, but is suitable for any pond if planted in a container.

Aponogeton distachyos, the water hawthorn, is an amazing water plant that flowers from spring or early summer right through until ice covers the surface of the pond. Its white flowers are slightly fragrant.

PLANTS FOR SHALLOW MARGINS
"Marginal" plants are grown with only a few centimetres of water above their crowns. They are often planted on special marginal shelves around the edge of the pond, about 23cm (9in) below the water. Try *Acorus gramineus* 'Variegatus', *Caltha palustris* (marsh marigold), *Pontederia cordata* (pickerel weed) and *Veronica beccabunga* (brooklime).

Acorus gramineus 'Variegatus' can be grown with an inch or so of water above the soil, and has the merit of being semi-evergreen. The flowers are insignificant and it is grown for foliage effect.

OXYGENATING PLANTS
Few of these submerged plants enhance the pond visually, but they are invaluable for the health of the pond if you keep fish. They

Myriophyllum aquaticum is one of the most attractive oxygenating plants because it produces some of its feathery foliage above the water. It's also useful for masking off the edge of the pond.

increase the oxygen content of the water when the fish most need it, and by absorbing nutrients they may also help to control the algae that cause green water.

Lagarosiphon major (also known as *Elodea crispa*) is one of the best known but it's a rampant grower and may have to be thinned out periodically. The water milfoils or myriophyllums are some of the most attractive oxygenators because much of their feathery growth rises above the surface.

BOG PLANTS

Bog plants grow in mud or wet soil that does not dry out but is not permanently submerged. Some will also survive in normal border soil, others will soon die if the ground dries out. Many primulas, such as *Primula japonica* and *P. bulleyana*, make excellent bog plants, but the skunk cabbage (*Lysichiton americanus*), with its strange yellow spathes, is one of the most spectacular in spring.

Primula bulleyana is one of several excellent bog species, especially beautiful when planted in drifts to maximize the full impact of the flowers when they come out in spring. It needs damp soil to thrive.

EASY ALPINES

Some of the easiest alpines, such as aubrieta and *Alyssum saxatile* (now more correctly called *Aurinia saxatilis*), are also the most rampant. Plant them for a bright display, but not in close proximity to choice but less rampant growers. Snow-in-summer (*Cerastium tomentosum*) falls into the same category. The rock phloxes *Phlox subulata* and *P. douglasii*, along with many of the spring-flowering saxifrages, are examples of rock plants that make a bold show even from a distance but are not so invasive.

Phlox douglasii varieties produce sheets of colour in the rock garden in spring. This variety is 'Daniel's Cushion'. Although these plants form a carpet of growth, they are easy to control.

CHOICE ALPINES

There are so many choice alpines, both widely available and uncommon, that any selection must reflect personal preferences. Two that are definitely worth including, not only for their deep blue colour but also because they flower after the main flush of spring, are *Gentiana septemfida* (mid- to late summer) and *G. sino-ornata* (early to mid-autumn).

Gentiana septemfida is especially useful for colour in the rock garden in late summer and, since the foliage is evergreen, provides some winter interest too. It requires a humus-rich soil to do really well.

DWARF CONIFERS

Not everyone appreciates dwarf conifers and in a very small rock garden they may look out of place. However, they give it structure and interest in winter. One that's small enough even for an alpine trough is *Juniperus communis* 'Compressa', which makes a miniature column of grey-green foliage. If there's space, some of the larger ones are bright, including *J. communis* 'Depressa Aurea' and *Thuja orientalis* 'Aurea Nana'.

Juniperus communis 'Compressa' is one of the best dwarf conifers for a rock garden. It is relatively slow growing and even an old plant is unlikely to exceed about 75cm (2½ft) in height.

GARDENING FOR WILDLIFE

....

For many of us, wildlife such as birds and butterflies add immeasurably to the delights of gardening, bringing not only colour and beauty but birdsong too. Even the less spectacular wildlife, like insects and beetles, plays a vital role in pollinating flowers and fruit, and many act as a natural form of pest control.

Gardens designed purely with wildlife in mind can look uninspiring – even weedy if you encourage butterfly food plants such as nettles. The long grass and seeding wild flowers that attract such a diversity of wildlife may not be your idea of a neat garden. With compromise, however, it is possible to have the best of both worlds, especially if you give over only part of the garden to the wild flowers and long grass, and incorporate water features and plenty of shrubs and evergreen climbers in the more conventional parts of the garden, with flower borders that also include insect-attracting plants.

■ ABOVE
A birdbath or feeder is one of the simplest ways to attract wildlife.

■ OPPOSITE
An unremarkable garden in terms of size and shape has become a refuge for local wildlife. Borders densely planted with shrubs, and a few trees, offer shelter for many kinds of insects and animals as well as birds.

INSPIRATIONAL IDEAS

Simple structures, like nesting boxes and bird tables or feeding nets, will encourage plenty of birds, and even the compost heap and wood pile may afford the shelter and protection that many overwintering animals and insects require.

■ ABOVE
Wildlife will be attracted to a garden with lots of trees, shrubs and ground-cover plants, which will provide hiding places for birds, insects and other wildlife. Insects are an important link in the food chain and will in turn attract plenty of birds to the garden.

■ ABOVE
Anyone lucky enough to garden in the
countryside starts off at an advantage,
and often it is sufficient to grow plenty
of cottage-garden plants and to provide
sufficient cover and a supply of water, to
encourage wildlife into your garden.

■ RIGHT
A wildlife haven can be created even in a
very small front garden. Here, a bog
garden has been built in place of a
border, which has deliberately been left
rather wild, with a small pond at the end.
This attracts not only frogs, toads,
newts, and spectacular dragonflies and
damsel-flies, but a whole range of insects
and small mammals. Such refuges are
really worthwhile in small town gardens
where natural habitats are increasingly
under threat.

145

INSPIRATIONAL IDEAS

Gardening with wildlife in mind does not necessarily mean a wild-looking garden, just a balance of features that in total make your garden a nature-friendly place. Set aside parts of the garden for wildlife so you can have the best of both worlds.

■ ABOVE

A suburban or town garden can support a surprising amount of wildlife if it is planned with a good mix of trees, shrubs and open space. Putting out food for birds and other local wildlife, and planting flowers that attract butterflies and other insects will also ensure a garden packed with activity and interest.

■ OPPOSITE

Woodland gardens, especially those with open spaces as well as plenty of trees, will usually encourage a wide range of wildlife. Trees alone do not make a garden, however, so lawns and other open areas are important to introduce some sense of design and to encourage those creatures that prefer more open spaces.

■ RIGHT
Borders with lots of flowers will certainly attract bees, butterflies, and all kinds of insect life. Retaining a nettle patch in an unobtrusive position, perhaps at the back of a shed or boundary bank, for the caterpillars of attractive butterflies, need not mean a garden that looks neglected or lacking in colour. Some of the best wildlife gardens are a compromise between the wild and the beautiful.

Know-how
WAYS WITH WATER

Wildlife gardening is a compromise between creating a garden that we find aesthetically pleasing and one which wildlife finds attractive. Often these demands are in conflict, but with a little imagination it's possible to combine both aims.

Water is a magnet for wildlife of all kinds, not just amphibians and aquatics. For those with children, there are some simple, safe water features that will provide an opportunity for wildlife to visit to drink and bathe. Even a birdbath is better than no water at all.

■ BELOW
PONDS A pond like this makes an attractive feature in its own right, and can form the centrepiece around which the garden is designed, but it will also bring the bonus of wildlife that otherwise would not visit the area.
DESIGN TIP *An informally shaped pond with easy access from the edges is more likely to attract wildlife than a formal one which is difficult to reach.*

■ ABOVE

STREAMS Anyone lucky enough to have a natural stream running through their garden is fortunate indeed, and will almost certainly have plenty of visiting wildlife. For those less fortunate, it's possible to create a very convincing man-made stream like this one.

DESIGN TIP *To make an artificial stream look truly convincing, plant densely up to the water's edge, using plenty of native plants.*

■ ABOVE

SMALL WATER FEATURES Everyone has space for a simple wildlife water feature like this. It's only an old dustbin (trashcan) lid filled with pebbles and placed over a reservoir with a small pump that recirculates the water through the frog's mouth. Although it won't support amphibians or insect life, it will make a water hole for birds and many mammals.

DESIGN TIP *Use this kind of feature to bring movement and life to an otherwise dull part of the garden, perhaps in a very shady spot where few plants thrive.*

■ RIGHT

BANKS Don't be afraid to use native plants and garden plants together if it helps to create the right illusion. This pond bank has a very natural appearance despite being planted with many cultivated plants.

DESIGN TIP *The larger the expanse of water, the more important it is to plant the banks imaginatively unless it is intended to create a void or texture within a formal setting.*

Know-how
WILDFLOWER MEADOWS

Gardens recently created on grassland already rich in wild flowers are likely to have lots of flowers germinating everywhere. Elsewhere, it may be necessary to introduce them. There are companies that specialize in wildflower seeds (as separate species and as mixtures), and you can even buy young plants from some nurseries and specialist suppliers.

■ LEFT

WILD AREAS If the lawn is large enough, it's possible to have ornamental areas to enjoy as a traditional lawn, while in other areas the grass is left to grow long and wild flowers are allowed to seed naturally. In this garden, wild orchids are among the flowers that thrive in the unmown areas. Such diversity of flowers attracts a wide selection of butterflies and birds.

DESIGN TIP *For a more "sculptured" effect, a large lawn can be cut to several different heights, the shortest grass forming paths and broad drives through the taller zones.*

■ RIGHT

MEADOW MIXTURES This sown meadow mixture has a diversity of grasses and broad-leaved plants. Although mixtures where one type of plant predominate are often more spectacular for a short time, a wider range of plants may be more useful for attracting wildlife and may sustain flowering over a longer period.

DESIGN TIP *Meadow mixtures are intended for sowing in place of a lawn where there's room for a decidedly "wild" garden. They seldom look right in juxtaposition with more conventional beds and borders.*

■ LEFT

NATIVE PLANTS Wild and woodland areas can sometimes be left uncultivated in large gardens. They will be colonized by native plants some of which can be very decorative. The self-seeded red campion (*Silene dioica*) shown here is native to the area where this photograph was taken.

DESIGN TIP *These truly wild areas may look stunning for a relatively short time, and uninspiring at other seasons. For that reason they are appropriate only for the fringes of a very large garden.*

■ RIGHT

WILD BORDERS This group of wild flowers, allowed to grow as a natural drift between lawn and border, shows how colourful wild flowers can be. Later in the season, when they grow tall and untidy, they can be cut back to make the area tidier.

DESIGN TIP *Avoid positioning this kind of wild bank in a conspicuous place. It will be more acceptable tucked away in a quiet part of the garden, something wildlife will also appreciate.*

■ LEFT

CULTIVATED WILD FLOWERS Cultivated wild flowers have transformed an otherwise waste piece of ground into an eye-catching feature that is as bright and colourful as many carefully planted borders. Several seed companies offer wildflower mixtures, and some specialize in wildflower seeds.

DESIGN TIP *Use wild flowers to brighten up an uninteresting bank or strip of vacant land. These have been sown on a railway (railroad) embankment at the end of a garden, but the location could just as well be a roadside verge.*

Know-how

ORCHARDS AND WOODS

Open woodland and orchards make ideal wildlife sanctuaries, and they form a natural transition between the formal parts of the garden and the truly wild areas.

■ ABOVE
UNDERPLANTING Woodland is not always dark and dreary – bluebells are among several woodland plants that spread readily once introduced. Cultivated bulbs like the tulips and muscari shown here can also be used, provided the shade is not too dense. If you have a large garden, a woodland area will make an ideal wildlife retreat.
DESIGN TIP *If you are planting a new woodland, birches are quick-growing and, being deciduous, are ideal for under-planting with spring-flowering plants. These make most growth before the leaves of deciduous trees cast too much shade.*

BE OPEN

Open areas within woodland or around the edge are likely to have the greatest variety of wildlife and wild flowers. You don't require a very large garden, or need to think too long-term, to establish a small woodland glade or a copse. Choose quick-growing trees such as birch, especially *Betula pendula*, which can reach over 6m (20ft) in a decade, and space them out well so that they retain an attractive shape and do not cast too much shade. A small copse of about a dozen trees within a large lawn can be very appealing and provide excellent shelter for many types of wildlife.

■ LEFT
PATIOS
Woodland areas need not be positioned away from the house. A wild area near a patio looks charming, and will attract wildlife close to your door. Proximity to wildlife can be a blessing, but be prepared for unwanted intruders.
DESIGN TIP *Leave the edges of wildlife beds as natural-looking as possible.*

KEEPING IT TRIM If you have a large garden with space for an orchard, or a woodland area, you have the potential for an ideal wildlife habitat. Allow wild flowers to take over most of the area – the long grass can be cut only once or twice a year (provided there are no rare plants to be considered) to keep the area presentable. Just mow the grass paths regularly.
DESIGN TIP *Paths can be either straight or meandering. Aim to make the path natural- looking – not mown too closely, or trimmed too geometrically.*

■ RIGHT
WILDFLOWER ORCHARD Once part of an old orchard, this area is now studded with *Fritillaria meleagris* and wood anemones (*Anemone nemorosa*) along with daffodils. All these plants naturalize well in grassed orchards, and look very pretty in spring. Summer wild flowers continue the display, and wildlife is always abundant in this environment.
DESIGN TIP *Don't wait for nature to transform an old orchard. Be prepared to naturalize bulbs and plant or sow wild flowers if appropriate.*

Know-how

FEATHERED FRIENDS

Of all the wildlife that visits the garden, birds are perhaps the most ready to respond to a little coaxing. They will soon become regular visitors if you routinely leave out suitable food, and some may also become relatively tame. They also appreciate water, for drinking and bathing, and this too will ensure they return frequently.

■ ABOVE

ORNAMENTAL BIRD TABLES
Bird tables are usually practical rather than ornamental, but it doesn't have to be that way. This home-made bird house is an ornamental feature in its own right, though the finer points will probably be lost on the birds.

DESIGN TIP *Position a bird table where cats and other animals can't jump up on to it, but try to avoid the centre of the lawn if possible. Bird tables and bird houses soon begin to weather and can quickly become unattractive if left covered with unsightly droppings.*

■ ABOVE

DOVECOTE A dovecote should ensure the company of some elegant feathered friends, and it can become a charming ornamental feature in its own right.

DESIGN TIP *Dovecotes are often painted white and placed in a conspicuous part of the lawn, but they may look better sited towards the back of a border.*

■ OPPOSITE BELOW

BIRDBATHS: ADDING INTEREST
A birdbath simply placed in isolation on the lawn can look a little stark. Making an attractive base such as this one, which has alpines planted in the gravel, makes a more powerful focal point.

DESIGN TIP *Don't assume the centre of the lawn is the best place for a birdbath. It will often look more pleasing if it is placed to one side or not far from the edge of the lawn and close to a border. It will draw the eye across the garden, and birds may feel more secure with the shelter of trees and shrubs nearby.*

■ ABOVE

BIRDBATHS Birdbaths can help to
break up a border and sustain interest at
those times of the year when herbaceous
plants are not at peak performance.
Although birdbaths are frequently
placed as focal points in a more formal
setting, or within the lawn, in some
styles of garden a border position may
be more appropriate.

DESIGN TIP *Try planting a ground
cover around the base of the pedestal to
make it look a more integrated part of the
design. When the border is bare, evergreen
ground cover is particularly useful.*

Planning and Planting
A SANCTUARY GARDEN

This garden is a sanctuary for wildlife of many kinds, but it's also a place where the gardener can retreat from the pressures of everyday life. It is a combination of wild and formal.

Three elements that are strongly attractive to many kinds of wildlife are woodland shelter, water and plenty of flowers rich in nectar and pollen. This garden is designed to provide all three.

As woodland adjoins the property, part of the garden boundary has been merged into the wooded area, and water has been introduced for the benefit of gardener and wildlife alike.

The pergola acts as a kind of natural bridge between the canopy of trees and the island beds. Although it's tempting to plant

PLANNING

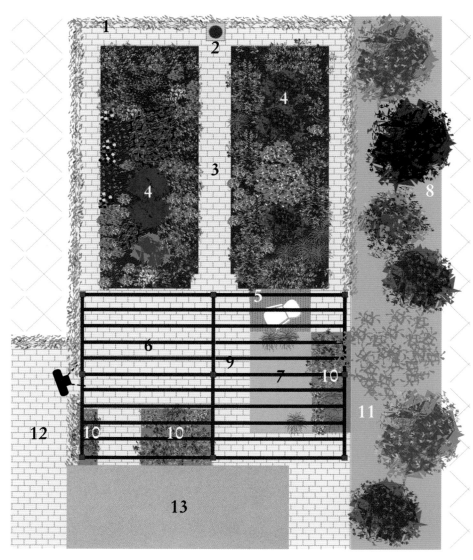

lots of wild flowers, in a garden like this, with a fairly rigid structure, it's best to concentrate on cultivated ornamentals that can be enjoyed by insects because they are rich in nectar or pollen. Although many annuals, and some outstanding herbaceous perennials, are ideal attractants, shrubs are essential to prevent the beds looking flat and uninteresting in winter. If you include berried shrubs such as cotoneasters, these will provide a source of food for birds in autumn and winter.

The adjoining woodland area provides the necessary shelter for wildlife of many kinds, but areas of long grass also ensure many kinds of wild flowers thrive that would be unable to survive in a closely mown lawn. These in turn will attract insects and birds.

PLANTING

ISLAND BORDERS

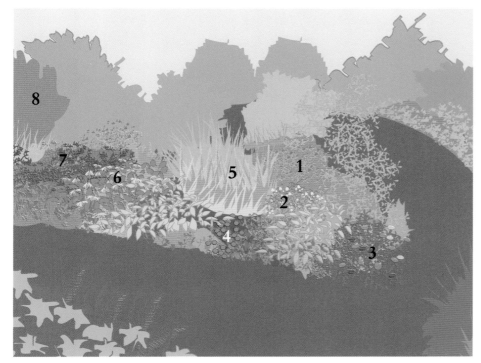

ISLAND BORDERS Island beds are useful design elements for breaking up large spaces. They also look attractive from all sides. The two island beds in

the plan opposite have four "faces", each offering a different perspective and groupings of plants. Island beds can be formal in shape, as shown in the plan opposite, or informal in outline, as

KEY TO PLANTS

1 *Salvia guaranitica*
2 *Polygonatum* x *hybridum*
3 *Osteospermum jucundum*
4 *Origanum laevigatum* 'Herrenhausen'
5 *Iris pseudacorus* 'Variegata'
6 *Ligularia dentata*
7 *Persicaria amplexicaulis* 'Atrosanguinea'
8 *Cornus alba* 'Aurea'

in the illustration on the left. Large borders can be filled with herbaceous plants and bulbs, and benefit from the inclusion of a few shrubs. Even if they are not evergreen, the framework of stems gives height to the border in winter. Some flowering shrubs, such as hydrangeas, will look more interesting if the old flower heads are allowed to remain until the following spring.

Shrubs with colourful winter stems, such as *Cornus stolonifera* 'Flaviramea' and *Cornus alba* 'Sibirica' also help to sustain interest throughout the seasons.

Planning and Planting
WILD FORMALITY

The conflict between the needs of wildlife, which prefers a largely uncultivated area, and the gardener's desire for an attractive formal garden has been reconciled in this design.

PLANNING

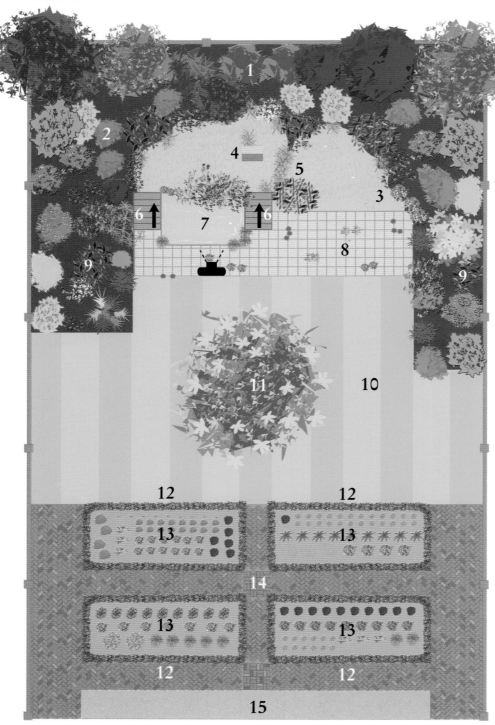

Two distinct parts of the garden have been linked by a lawn and a large weeping tree. The tree acts as a midway focal point to assist the gradual transition that marries these two contrasting styles: a formal herb garden near to the house, with a wildlife area of rough grass, pond, shrubs and trees at the far end of the garden.

Wildlife areas can sometimes look overgrown and weedy. That's how things are in nature, but not necessarily how we like our gardens to look. You can have the best of both worlds by making the end of the garden a wildlife zone, while retaining a more formal style near to the house. A lawn is a good way of linking the two styles; rough grass with wild flowers at the back, and a formal, neatly mown lawn nearer to the house.

PLANTING

Added interest has been created in the brick paving around the formal beds by using two different bonding patterns.

RANDOM PAVING

The term random paving is a misnomer, as it actually needs to be carefully planned. A very regular pattern, where the slabs all align, can look a bit repetitive, especially when covering large areas. Staggering them, and perhaps using slabs of different sizes, will add character and interest. If you wish to plant in the crevices, between the paving, either leave large gaps unmortared, or space the slabs to leave a larger planting area.

Natural stone always looks particularly pleasing when laid in a random pattern, but you can also buy concrete slabs of different sizes to achieve a similar effect. The latter are readily available and generally less expensive.

HOW TO LAY RANDOM PAVING

1 Excavate your chosen area to a depth that will allow for about 5cm (2in) of compacted hardcore (rubble) topped with approximately 5cm (2in) of ballast (sand and gravel), plus the thickness of the paving stones.

2 Place five blobs of mortar where the slab is to be placed, one in the centre, the others near the corners. Alternatively, cover the area where the paving is to be laid with mortar, ensuring it is fairly level.

3 Bed the slab on the mortar and check with a spirit level. If laying a large area, lay on a slight slope to ensure water runs off freely. Use a wedge of wood under one end of the spirit level to check the slope.

4 *(right)* Use spacers of an even thickness to ensure regular spacing, and adjust the slabs again if necessary. If you are planning to plant in the crevices, leave large spaces between the paving. Remove the spacers before filling the joints with mortar. Wait

for a day or two before mortaring the joints. Use a dryish mortar mix, and with a small trowel push it well down between the joints. Finish off with a smooth stroke, leaving the mortar slightly recessed. Wipe any stains off the slabs before the mortar dries.

Planning and Planting
SQUARING UP TO THE PROBLEM

This garden successfully marries a formal garden with the informality of a wildlife area. A formal geometric-based design is combined with a woodland space accommodating the needs of both wildlife and gardener.

Woodland gardens make excellent wildlife refuges, but they can be unstimulating to look out on to

from the house. This garden retains a strong sense of design in the area immediately in front of

PLANNING

the house, combining differently shaped rectangles and squares, with the wildlife area containing rough grass and trees running along one side. Being at the edge of an area that contains some large trees, it receives a lot of shade, but the strong sense of line and the different surface textures used in the formal area ensure the garden always looks interesting, with many shade-tolerant foliage plants playing an important role.

Water always attracts wildlife, so a small pool has been included, with a shallow sloping beach at one end for a bathing area for birds.

PRE-FORMED PONDS
Your design may require a small informally shaped pool, and a pre-formed pond is a quick and easy solution. If the ponds are displayed on their sides, lay them on the ground before buying as they may look smaller from a normal viewing position.

PLANTING

HOW TO INSTALL A PRE-FORMED POND

1 Transfer your shape to the ground by inserting canes around the edge of the pond. Run a hosepipe (garden hose) or rope around the outside of the canes.

2 Remove the pond and canes and excavate the hole to approximately the required depth, following the profile of the shelves as accurately as possible.

3 Place a straight-edged piece of wood across the rim of the hole to check that it is level. Measure down to confirm that you have dug to the required depth.

4 Put the pond in the hole, then add or remove soil to ensure a snug and level fit. Remove any large stones. Check with a spirit level that the pond is level.

5 *(right)* Remove the pond, then line the excavation with damp sand if the soil is stony. With the pond in position, and levels checked again, backfill with sand or fine soil, being careful not to push the pond out of level.

6 *(right)* Fill with fresh water from a hose pipe and backfill further if necessary as the water rises, checking the levels frequently as backfilling often lifts the pond slightly. The pond is now ready to fill with plants and wildlife.

Planning and Planting

WILD AND WONDERFUL

A large garden in an attractive setting offers every opportunity for a really superb display that's pleasing for the gardener and an ideal habitat for many kinds of wildlife. The sloping ground on which this garden has been constructed offers plenty of scope for attractive landscaping.

Large gardens with a natural slope must be designed to make use of the natural contours of the land

wherever possible. For this reason, gardens like this are almost always unique. However, you can take the

KEY TO PLAN

1 Coniferous woodland
2 Woodland
3 Grass path
4 Steps
5 Ornamental trees, shrubs and herbaceous planting
6 Grass
7 Bridge
8 Stream
9 Balustrade
10 Pergola over entrance to steps
11 Lawn (level)
✕ Garden continues
↓ Direction of steps down
⚲ Viewpoint on photograph

PLANNING

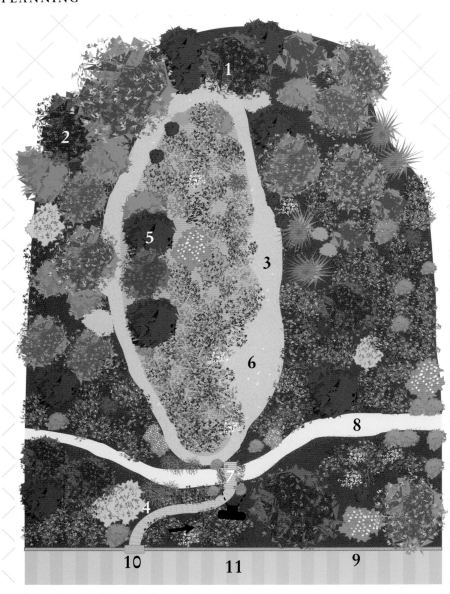

general principles and design concepts to apply to your own garden, if it seems appropriate. Although this is a large garden, a smaller sloping site could be landscaped in a similar way.

A natural stream is a tremendous asset to any garden, but with a little ingenuity and a lot of energy you can make an artificial stream using a liner.

■ OPPOSITE
PLANTING IN DRY SHADE Wooded areas are always more attractive if they are underplanted with herbaceous plants and dwarf shrubs. The shady area beneath trees is often dry, however, so choose plants that can tolerate those conditions, and be sure to keep them well watered for the first season until they become established.

It may help to remove some of the lower branches of large trees (this is best done by a tree surgeon, who may also be able to thin the crown if it's necessary).

To keep woodland looking natural, use curved paths and not straight ones, and allow some of the plants to tumble over the edge. If planting a large area, individual plants may have little impact, in which case plant in drifts of the same kind of plant.

PLANTING

PLANTS FOR DRY SHADE

KEY TO PLANTS

1 *Ajuga reptans*
2 *Geranium magnificum*
3 *Geranium pratense*
4 *Deutzia* x *kalmiiflora*
5 *Rubus spectabilis* 'Flore Pleno'
6 *Geranium macrorrhizum* 'Album'
7 *Colchicum autumnale*
8 *Arum italicum*
9 *Myosotis sylvatica*
10 *Helleborus* hybrids
11 *Geranium macrorrhizum*
12 *Galium odoratum* (syn. *Asperula odorata*)

Planning and Planting
NATURE TRAILS

Where the garden is large enough to create an area devoted to informal walkways, which can meander between and around small streams, woodland and meadow-type grassed patches, the result can look very natural.

PLANNING

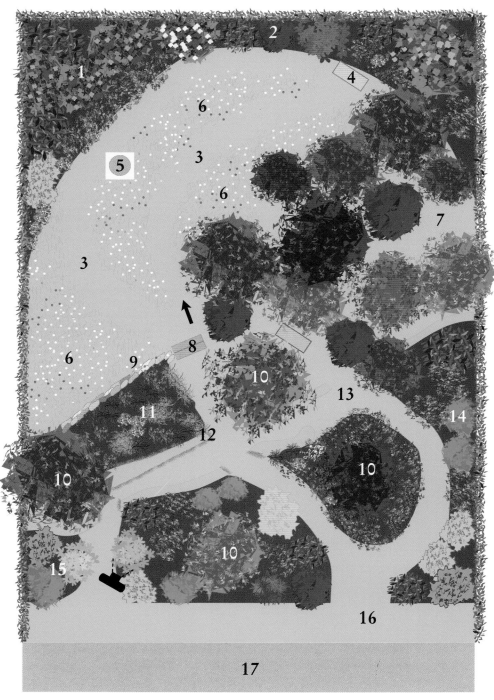

KEY TO PLAN

1 Specimen shrubs
2 Mixed border planted mainly with plants that attract butterflies and other wildlife
3 Mown grass path
4 Garden bench
5 Large sculpture or ornament
6 Rough grass with wild flowers
7 Woodland garden
8 Steps
9 Stone wall
10 Specimen tree
11 Bog garden
12 Stream
13 Grass paths
14 Mixed bed
15 Shrubs
16 Lawn
17 House
↑ Direction of steps down
⚲ Viewpoint on photograph

Although this garden appears to consist mainly of meandering paths that look perfectly natural, they have been planned for maximum impact. Apart from the point where the paths converge at the steps between wooded and open areas, paths split and merge, or go around in loops. This layout offers multiple choices for exploring the garden. The wildlife it attracts will be equally varied, with trees, water, long grass and wild flowers providing a wide range of habitats. The borders are planted mainly with flowers that attract insects and shrubs that provide birds with berries.

PLANTING

DECORATIVE DECKCHAIRS

■ ABOVE

In an informal garden like the one opposite, deckchairs are ideal for taking out on a sunny day for relaxing amid the wild flowers and birdsong. If you have old deckchairs that have seen better days, it's easy to give them a new lease of life by covering them with new canvas and getting to work with some stencil paints. You will need about 1.5m (5ft) of deckchair canvas, which should be washed, rinsed, dried and ironed before use.

You can buy stencils from art supply shops, or you can make your own, to stencil both canvas and surround. Alternatively, try staining the old wood with a coloured woodstain to co-ordinate or contrast with the decorated canvas.

■ ABOVE

Work out your design first, then fix the stencil in position using masking tape. Load the stencil brush with paint, removing any excess paint by dabbing up and down on a piece of newspaper, then apply the colour to the relevant part of the stencil. Move the stencil and repeat until all areas of that colour have been painted. Then reposition the stencil over the original colour and apply a fresh paint colour. Repeat until the design is complete. When dry, set the paint by covering it with a white cloth and pressing with an iron at its hottest setting, covering each part for at least two minutes. Use upholstery tacks to fix the canvas securely to the top and bottom of the chair.

Planning and Planting
MERGING WITH THE LANDSCAPE

A large garden in a rural setting can merge into the landscape if the boundaries are planted with shrubs and trees, rather like the edge of a woodland area. A garden of this size will have a lot of lawn, but by leaving some areas long for wild flowers and wildlife, the amount of time spent on maintenance is reduced.

PLANNING

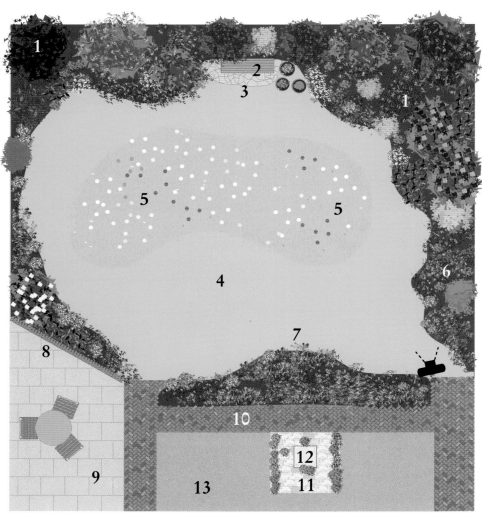

KEY TO PLAN

1 Tree and shrub border
2 Garden seat
3 Paved area around seat
4 Lawn
5 Long grass and wild flowers
6 Shrubs and ground cover
7 Low-growing shrubs
8 Retaining wall
9 Patio
10 Brick paving
11 Courtyard of natural stone paving and dwarf shrubs
12 Formal pond
13 House

Viewpoint on photograph

of the house. Although small, it is a secluded area that will be visited by plenty of wildlife, including birds, which will use it for drinking and bathing.

The slightly elevated large patio gives a good view across the garden, and emphasizes that this is a garden for relaxation and enjoyment rather than weeding and work.

INTRODUCING WILD FLOWERS TO THE GARDEN
You can encourage birds, butterflies and other creatures by having a wildflower lawn, instead of a grass lawn. You may still want to retain a grass lawn for practical purposes, but parts of it can be allowed to "go wild", especially parts that are well screened. If your lawn doesn't already contain plenty of wild flowers (or weeds), you can sow a seed mixture, or for a small area you can plant them as wild-flower plants.

Despite its large size, this garden has been planned for minimum work and maximum enjoyment. Cutting the grass is the only tedious chore, but leaving areas of grass long for wild flowers and wildlife reduces the area to be mown regularly, and a large

powered mower can make short work of it. There are few seasonal plants in containers to be watered, and the trees and shrubs require no regular maintenance.

A small, formal pond has been introduced into the courtyard-like paved area between the two wings

PLANTING

SOWING AND PLANTING WILD FLOWERS

1 The most satisfactory way to create a wildflower lawn is to sow a special wildflower mixture instead of lawn seed. Be careful to clear the ground of problem perennial weeds before you start.

2 To bury the seeds, simply rake first in one direction and then in the other. It does not matter if some seeds remain on the surface. Keep the area well watered until the seeds germinate. Protect from birds if necessary.

3 For a very small area, you may prefer to buy wild-flower plants. You can raise your own from seed or buy them. They are available from specialist nurseries and some garden centres.

4 You can plant into bare ground or put them in an existing lawn left to grow long. Remember to keep them well watered until established.

Choosing Plants
PLANTS FOR WILDLIFE

Most plants help to attract wildlife in some form, but some are especially good at enticing particular types. *Buddleia davidii*, for example, is also called the butterfly bush because these creatures find it so irresistible. Nepetas are usually buzzing with bees.

SHRUBS FOR BUTTERFLIES

The butterfly bush (*Buddleia davidii*) has to be high on the list, but remember the other buddleias, such as *B. alternifolia* and *B. globosa*. Other shrubs popular with butterflies include ceanothus, heathers, many hebes, lavender, and *Spiraea* x *bumalda* (now more correctly *S. japonica*).

Buddleia davidii is sometimes called the butterfly bush, because butterflies are so strongly attracted by it. It's very easy to grow, even on poor soils, but regular pruning is necessary to keep the plant compact. There are varieties in shades of blue, purple, pink and white.

BORDER PLANTS FOR BUTTERFLIES

These border plants are as irresistible to butterflies as the best of the shrubs. Some of these flower late, which is a bonus in the garden, among them most of the perennial asters, such as *A. amellus*, *A.* x *frikartii*, *A. novae-angliae*, *A. novi-belgii* and *Sedum spectabile* and its hybrids.

Sedum spectabile will bring a border to life in autumn, and be the centre of attraction among the local population of bees and butterflies. There are several good varieties. This one is 'Meteor'.

ANNUALS FOR BUTTERFLIES

Many summer annuals, such as pansies and French marigolds, will also attract butterflies. Others that are particularly popular with them include ageratum, candytuft and *Alyssum maritimum* (now more correctly *Lobularia maritima*).

French marigolds are excellent garden plants, flowering from early summer until the first frost if dead-headed, and attract butterflies throughout the season. This variety is 'Red Cherry'.

PLANTS FOR CATERPILLARS

Caterpillars sometimes require totally different plants from butterflies for their food, and the availability of these significantly determines the local population. The fact that butterflies usually lay their eggs on different plants (and often weeds) from the plants they feed on for nectar is a great

Nasturtiums (*Tropaeolum majus*) are cheerful and easy-to-grow hardy annuals, but some butterfly species lay their eggs on the leaves. For that reason this is a mixed-blessings plant, as the caterpillars could become a pest that you then have to control.

consolation for the gardener, otherwise they would not be so welcome in the garden. Stinging nettles (*Urtica dioica*) are popular with many species, and some feed on thistles. Among the ornamental garden plants that are eaten by caterpillars of some species are nasturtiums (*Tropaeolum majus*) and canary creeper (*Tropaeolum peregrinum*).

Butterflies are sometimes very specific about the plants on which they lay their eggs, however, so in some countries other plants may be preferred to suit local species. If you are keen to encourage butterflies, consult books on the subject that give advice on which food plants to provide.

MOTHS IN THE NIGHT

Night-flying moths, and other night-flying insects, are not everyone's idea of creatures that will beautify the garden, but for anyone interested in wildlife of all kinds, insects that come out at dusk can be equally exciting. These are generally attracted by night-scented plants such as some of the nicotianas and night-scented stocks (*Matthiola bicornis*, now more correctly *M. longipetala*).

Evening-flowering nicotianas will attract insects such as night-flying moths. They are usually very fragrant too, which is a bonus for us. Many of the modern hybrids have been bred to open during the day, so check in the catalogue or on the packet if you want one that flowers in the evening.

FOR THE BIRDS

Birds are attracted by nesting sites and food plants. Dense climbers and evergreen hedges provide nesting sites for many species. Birds that eat mainly seeds are likely to be enticed by plants such as teasels (*Dipsacus fullonum* and *D. sativus*), which have large seed heads, while birds that enjoy berries will be encouraged into the garden by many *Sorbus* species as well as pyracanthas.

Pyracanthas are grown primarily for their berries. The birds will leave them alone at first, but they often provide a useful meal when severe weather arrives.

GOOD BEE PLANTS

If you're a bee-keeper, or are simply fascinated by these industrious insects, plants that attract bees will be high on your planting list. On the other hand, if you regard them as unpleasant insects with a nasty sting, you may prefer to avoid such plants.

Catmint (*Nepeta racemosa*, still widely sold under its older name of *N. mussinii*, and *N.* x *faassenii*) and marjorams are among the plants especially attractive to bees, but so are many other summer border flowers, such as the hardy

Nepeta x *faassenii* is a lovely summer border plant, much-loved by bees. It may be best to avoid planting it where it will overhang a narrow path, to reduce the risk of being stung.

geraniums. For spring, include brooms (cytisus), aubrietia and crocuses, and for autumn the perennial asters listed for butterflies and *Sedum spectabile*.

FOR BENEFICIAL INSECTS

A diversity of flowers is the best way to attract beneficial insects (predators) to the garden, and annuals are especially useful. One of the best is the poached-egg plant (*Limnanthes douglasii*), with its pretty carpet of yellow and white flowers. Although an annual, it self-seeds readily.

Limnanthes douglasii is a bright and cheerful little annual that will usually self-seed itself to provide more plants the following year.

SMALL GARDENS

Size is relative when it comes to gardens, but most of us have a smaller one than we'd like. Not only do small gardens make it difficult to grow all the plants that tempt us, lack of space also tends to cramp our style when it comes to design. Even those fortunate enough to have a large back garden sometimes have a small front garden, and such restraints can seem limiting – especially if space for a drive has to be found.

There are as many solutions as there are gardens, but the illustrations and ideas that follow show that a small garden does not necessarily mean small impact. Even an unpromising, tiny, town front garden can be transformed with a little imagination. And, of course, some of the ideas shown for small gardens can be adapted for corners of a large one.

Boundaries also assume greater importance with a small garden. The fence, hedge or wall can dominate the view, whatever you do within the central planting area. It may be necessary to turn these to advantage, perhaps by erecting a decorative fence, such as a painted picket style, planting a dwarf flowering hedge or painting an existing wall a pale colour to reflect light and to act as a pleasing backdrop for wall shrubs and other plants.

■ ABOVE
A cottage-style front garden bursting with colour and fragrance.

■ OPPOSITE
Clever planting and design of this small town garden has created the
illusion of space.

INSPIRATIONAL IDEAS

A small garden can have just as striking an impact as a large expanse. Try to resist the temptation to overlook dramatic features or large plants. Bold statements are often most effective in small spaces, and a lot of small plants can draw attention to limited space.

■ OPPOSITE ABOVE

If a very small garden seems hemmed in by fences, turning the eye inwards towards the centre of the garden can be a good idea. The raised bed becomes the focal point from all parts of this tiny garden, drawing the eye inwards and away from the limitations of the boundary. Sufficient space was left at the end for a small sitting and barbecue area.

■ OPPOSITE BELOW

If your front garden is small, this example should convince you that there is plenty of scope for impact no matter how small the area. The Japanese-style entrance demonstrates effectively that shape and structure, together with colour, can be more important than the number of plants.

■ BELOW

A small back garden can have all the charm and elegance of a traditional garden more often associated with grand country houses. It's not only the formal structure of the garden but the strong white-and-silver theme that makes the whole design look well thought out and integrated. Picking up the colour in the paintwork of the gazebo and painting the central plinth white not only echoes the theme but ensures there is relief to the green of the surrounding trees and the box (*Buxus sempervirens*) hedges when the flowers have finished.

INSPIRATIONAL IDEAS

The vertical plane should be considered when making the most of small spaces. Tall features, such as birdbaths, can be useful to draw the eye upwards, as can vertical features such as high walls decorated with pots, or trellises clothed with climbers or painted brightly.

■ ABOVE

This narrow plot is typical of many small back gardens, and the straight path to the gate limits the scope without major reconstruction. It benefits greatly from having a gravel path instead of concrete slabs, which would have emphasized the rigidity of the path, and by training the hedge into an arch over the gate. The gate alone would not have been an attractive focal point, but the arch transforms it into an acceptable feature. Having the lawn at the top half of the garden and dense planting at the end, rather than running the lawn along the whole length of the garden, ensures the eye does not take in everything at once. Despite the limitation of size and shape, there is plenty to discover in this garden. The dense planting helps to overcome the lack of structural features.

■ OPPOSITE BELOW

Where space is very sparse, it's a good idea to extend a garden vertically. Although the ground area occupied by this garden is severely limited, the way it has been clothed from ground almost to first floor level has ensured that it is packed with colour and interest. Good use has been made of foliage plants so the display looks well clothed throughout the summer months.

■ ABOVE

Small country cottages and town houses with only a narrow strip of land between house and pavement (footway) or road can cramp the style of even the most enthusiastic garden designer. It may be best to abandon attempts at clever designs and concentrate on a mass of colourful annuals in summer and bulbs in spring. Window boxes and hanging baskets provide additional planting space and give the garden a vertical element, and with such a small garden the regular watering they require should not be an onerous chore.

Painting the wall almost always improves a small garden like this, and helps to show hanging baskets to maximum advantage.

Know-how
BEAUTIFUL BOUNDARIES

Unattractive walls and fences can be clothed with climbers and wall shrubs, but these may make a small area seem even more enclosed. If the view beyond the garden is an attractive one, it may be worth making a feature of the boundary itself.

■ RIGHT

PICKET FENCES Picket fences are always more attractive than a filled-in panel or closeboard fence. Normally they are left a natural wood colour or painted white, but why not be bold and splash out with the colours? One of these fences has been painted pastel pink to match the roses, the other sugar-almond blue to differentiate between the two properties.

DESIGN TIP *Bear in mind the colours of the flowers in adjoining borders, not only at the time of year when you paint the fence but throughout the rest of the year.*

■ ABOVE

FEATURE FENCE If you get on well with your neighbours, and you want to let in a little light, a fence with "windows" is one solution. Although you may want to modify the style to suit your own taste, the principle of making a feature of your fence is a useful one to bear in mind for a small garden.

DESIGN TIP *Fences look best if they are maintained at least annually with a fresh coat of preservative or paint. If you want to make a feature of your fence rather than mask it with climbers, be sure to allow for easy access for painting or preserving in your design, not obscuring it with large trees or shrubs.*

■ RIGHT

LIVING FENCE An existing solid fence can be improved by erecting a trellis in front of it and planting climbers such as clematis and roses. Here, a figure has been sited to bring a sense of summer enchantment, and also to provide a focal point in winter when the foliage cover has gone.

DESIGN TIP *If you find an exposed trellis unattractive in winter, include an evergreen such as ivy. But bear in mind that evergreens that twine through their support make maintenance of the trellis and fence difficult.*

■ BELOW

CAVITY WALLS Low walls are often better than tall ones for a small front garden, but plain single-skin walls can look drab and uninspiring. Building one with a cavity like this not only provides more planting space but also helps to bridge and link both sides of the garden boundary.

DESIGN TIP *Unless the boundary has to deter animals, a low wall or even a small-post-and-chain-link fence is effective. It is also possible to mark the boundary by planting up to the edge of a bed, which can be viewed from both sides.*

Know-how

INTEGRATING THE PRACTICALITIES

Planning should also involve practical essentials like somewhere to dry the washing and a hide for the dustbin (trashcan), as well as more stimulating features like a built-in barbecue. The most attractive garden can become an irritation if there's nowhere to dry the clothes or there's an inconvenient walk to put out the household refuse.

■ LEFT **CLOTHES DRIER** The only space for a clothes drier in this small garden was in the paved area shown. A rotary drier was chosen with the socket well hidden by beach pebbles where one of the paving slabs had been removed. This makes it possible to remove the drier when it is not in use, leaving the garden relatively unaffected by this necessity.
DESIGN TIP *Try to avoid a clothes line that runs straight down the garden, or across it at a conspicuous spot. Unless removed after use each time, it will visually divide the garden. Rotary driers can sometimes be masked completely by screen block walling in a convenient corner.*

BARBECUES Even if your use of the barbecue is infrequent, having one built in gives the impression of a garden well thought out and cleverly designed. All the racks and basic equipment can be bought as kits, so usually you only have to build the walls.

DESIGN TIP *Obtain specifications from kit manufacturers at the design stage. Armed with the dimensions of your preferred kit, it will be easier to integrate it into the brickwork or ensure that it's a good fit with the particular walling block that you are planning to use.*

■ BELOW

REFUSE This corner of a small garden can double as a built-in patio, barbecue or a refuse hide, depending on what's most applicable.

DESIGN TIP *Keep as many utilities as possible together in a small area if possible. This will minimize their impact on the rest of the garden.*

■ ABOVE

DRAINS Drain inspection covers sound mundane, but they are important where they occur in the middle of a crucial part of the garden, such as a patio or in the lawn. These metal covers immediately attract the eye, rather like an unattractive focal point, detracting from the more desirable elements. Special replacement covers that have a planting cavity or a shallow tray to hold paving are available. It is important to cut the paving accurately to ensure a neat appearance.

DESIGN TIP *Don't simply place a container over an inspection cover: it will almost certainly draw attention to the cover, which will probably project beneath the base of the container.*

Know-how

CREATING ILLUSIONS

Illusions are useful design devices, whatever the size of garden, but they are especially valuable in small ones. Mostly they are used to suggest that the garden is larger or more densely planted that it is in reality.

■ ABOVE

BEYOND THE DOOR Doors and gates suggest that it's possible to explore more of the garden. This large gate is clearly part of a garden on a grand scale, but you might be able to come to an arrangement with a neighbour to set a decorative gate between your two properties. If you are on friendly terms you can actually use it, otherwise agree to keep it locked. Both will benefit from the impression that the garden extends beyond its real limits.

DESIGN TIP *If using this kind of device, it's best if both gardens have a path leading to the gate, so that it really does look as though there's more garden to explore.*

■ LEFT

ENDLESS PATHS Dense planting with tall shrubs or trees at the end of a garden can suggest that the property goes further, even though the path turns or leads nowhere in particular. The effect works best in summer, when plants are in full leaf.

DESIGN TIP *A path will give the illusion of being longer if it tapers towards the far end. Dense planting at the perimeter of the garden also helps to imply there's more garden beyond.*

■ BELOW

DECEPTIVE TRELLIS Decorative trellis is usually more pleasing than a plain wall, and hints at things beyond.

DESIGN TIP *If using trellis ornamentally, do not over-plant and avoid covering it with climbers.*

Know-how

USING VERTICALS

In a large garden, the verticals are usually provided by trees, but in small gardens it is often the boundaries and house walls that obtrusively provide the vertical element. Arches, pergolas and trellises are useful for adding height within the garden, especially before newly planted small trees can play a useful role, but much can be achieved by covering existing walls and fences with climbers and wall shrubs.

■ LEFT
BUILT-UP BORDERS A small town or courtyard garden can appear almost claustrophobic, but it's possible to make a virtue of its enclosed nature by surrounding yourself with lush growth. Build up the borders all around to create a secret hideaway.
DESIGN TIP *This kind of planting works best if the borders have irregular outlines extending towards the centre, rather than straight, narrow borders. Use tubs to draw the eye into the centre. Use plenty of evergreens and variegated plants, and medium-sized with small plants towards the front of the border and climbers and tall plants at the back.*

■ OPPOSITE ABOVE

STYLISH SUPPORTS Climbing and rambling roses require a suitable support, and although wires can be stretched at intervals along the wall, a trellis is more decorative. This is especially useful if the wall itself is not particularly attractive as the trellis remains a feature even when the rose is bare.

DESIGN TIP *Try extending the trellis beyond the height of the wall or fence. This will produce a better display of roses and also ensure fewer thorny stems hanging where they could be a hazard.*

■ RIGHT

AVENUE OF ARCHES As most of the height was provided by the boundary and house walls, with a void in the centre, an ornate avenue of arches has been used to take the eye to the centre of the garden. It also creates a corridor linking two distinct areas of the garden. When the climbers have covered the frame, the tunnel effect will be emphasized.

DESIGN TIP *If the garden is small, it may be best to angle a pergola or arch to take the eye at an angle. This prevents the whole garden being absorbed at a glance.*

■ ABOVE

CLIMBERS AS CLOTHING Clothe the house wall whenever possible. Although the temptation is to use evergreens such as ivies, if the property is attractive in its own right, make use of seasonal flowering climbers such as roses and wisterias.

DESIGN TIP *Deciduous climbers such as roses are shown to advantage against a painted wall. Only those plants that can be lowered easily from the wall for periodic painting of the house are practical choices, however.*

■ ABOVE

COVERED IN CLIMBERS Clothing the lower level of a house will make the most of vertical space in a tiny garden. Here a colourful, evergreen *Euonymus fortunei* variety has been used beneath the window, and pyracanthas for greater height either side.

DESIGN TIP *Evergreens are a good choice for this kind of position, but use bright flowers near the base to pack a punch and give the garden colour.*

Planning and Planting
BEAUTIFUL BASEMENT

A small basement garden can be transformed into a delightful outdoor room like this, with a little planning and some clever planting. An advantage of a small space is the low cost: the expense is limited by the small amount you can pack in.

PLANNING

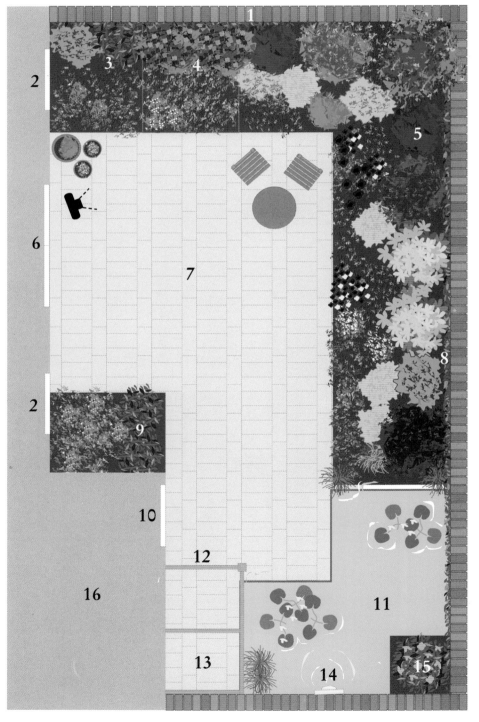

Basement gardens often seem unpromising at first – dark and uninteresting with little to bring cheer or admiration. But if you paint the walls white to reflect as much light as possible, add some raised beds to provide more impressive planting areas, install a pond with wall fountain, and buy some stylish garden furniture, then you have a garden packed with interest and impact.

In a small garden like this, accommodating practicalities such as the dustbin (trashcan) is always a problem. The best solution is to tuck the unsightly necessities away at the back where they will not be visible from seating areas. Washing lines can be replaced with a rotary drier, which can be stored when not in use. Dustbins can be tucked away in the alcove formed by the pergola.

PLANTING

RAISED BEDS

Bricks are a better choice than walling blocks for raised beds built close to the house. Even if a different kind of brick is used, it is likely to blend more harmoniously with the building than concrete or reconstituted stone blocks.

Bricklaying low walls is not a difficult skill to acquire, and the wall will go up surprisingly quickly once the footing has been prepared. You can always hire a professional if you don't have the time to build a wall yourself.

HOW TO BUILD A RAISED BED

1 All walls require a footing. For a low wall, the thickness of a single row of bricks is required. A double row of bricks is required for a taller wall. Excavate a trench about 30cm (1ft) deep, and place about 13cm (5in) of consolidated hardcore in the bottom. Drive pegs in so the tops are at the final height of the base. Use a spirit level to check levels.

2 Fill with a concrete mix of 1 part cement, 2 parts sharp sand, and 3 parts aggregate, and level it off with the peg tops. After the concrete has hardened (1–2 days) lay the bricks on a bed of mortar. Place a wedge of mortar at one end of each brick to be laid. For stability, make a pier at each end, and at intervals of 1.8–2.4m (6–8ft) if the wall is long.

3 For subsequent courses, lay a ribbon or mortar on top of the previous row, then "butter" one end of the brick to be laid. Tap level, checking constantly with a spirit level. The wall must be finished off with a coping of suitable bricks or with special coping sold for the purpose.

Planning and Planting
A PRIVATE GARDEN

Privacy can be important in a small garden, especially if it is overlooked by neighbouring properties. If you want seclusion, then planting plenty of tall evergreens around the perimeter will provide a sense of enclosure and privacy. Most of the design elements are then thrown towards the centre of the garden, so that the eye is taken inwards and the garden does not seem claustrophobic.

KEY TO PLAN

1	Conifer	8	Seasonal plants
2	Specimen ever-	9	Plants in pots
	green shrub	10	Patio
3	Ground cover	11	Seating area
4	Evergreen shrub	12	Crazy-paved
5	Gravel		patio
6	Planted	13	House
	container and		
	ornaments	![viewpoint]	Viewpoint on
7	Feature slab		photograph

This garden looks in on itself, with all the colour and bright plants running along the centre of the garden. The dense evergreen planting around the boundary and the use of conifers and other tall evergreens ensure a feeling of seclusion and privacy.

It is important to avoid a ribbon effect when a main path runs the length of the garden, so the path here has been broken up with decorative feature slabs, and patches of gravel take the eye outwards to the flowerbeds on either side. By mixing paving materials and taking the path out to the sides in an irregular manner, the eye is drawn to the planted areas and not just along the path.

TUBS AND POTS
The larger the pot or container, the more plants you can pack in and the more they are likely to thrive in the generous amount of potting soil.

PLANNING

PLANTING TUBS AND PATIO POTS

1 Filled tubs and pots can be heavy to move, so plant them up in their final positions if possible. Cover the drainage holes with a layer of broken pots, large gravel or chipped bark.

2 A loam-based potting mixture is best for most plants, but if the pot is to be used where weight is a consideration, such as on a balcony, use a peat-based or peat-substitute mixture.

3 Choose a tall or bold plant for the centre, such as *Cordyline australis* or a fuchsia, or one with large flowers such as the osteospermum that has been used here.

PLANTING

4 Fill in around the base with some bushier but lower-growing plants. Choose bright flowers if the centrepiece is a foliage plant, but place the emphasis on foliage effect if the focal point is a flowering plant.

5 Cover the surface with a decorative mulch such as chipped bark or cocoa shells if much of the surface is visible (this is worth doing anyway to conserve moisture). Water thoroughly.

Planning and Planting
WAYS WITH WALLS

The walls of a small enclosed garden can be oppressive, yet masking them with evergreen shrubs and conifers may emphasize the smallness. This design opens up the centre and uses decorative trellis to make a feature of the walls.

PLANNING

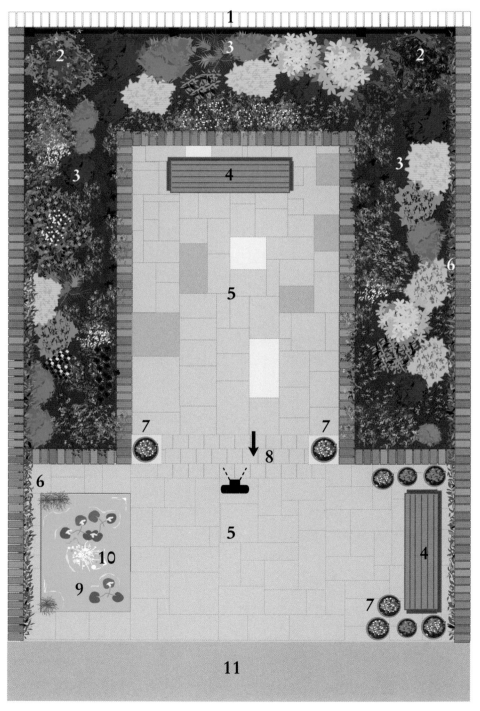

Decorative trellises ensure instant impact and will in time be covered with plants, preventing walls looking dull or oppressive. A white trellis looks good against a green backdrop of foliage, but don't be afraid to use a dark colour against a wall, especially if the wall is white or a light colour.

The raised beds in this design elevate the plants, so the boundary walls behind do not appear quite so high. Similarly, a change of level adds interest, but to relieve the possible dominance of the paving in the lower area a formal pond complete with fountain provides a focal point, especially when viewed from the garden seat on the opposite side.

WATER LILIES
Plant water lilies in spring, before the leaves have fully expanded. They can be planted in special planting baskets or in a container with solid sides, such as an old washing-up bowl.

PLANTING

HOW TO PLANT A WATER LILY

1 Use a heavy soil that is not too rich in nutrients. Aquatic planting soil is available from aquatic specialists.

2 Don't add ordinary fertilizers to the soil, as they may cause a proliferation of algae. Use a slow-release fertilizer.

3 Remove the water lily from its container, and plant it in the new container at its original depth.

4 Add a layer of gravel to reduce the chance of fish disturbing the soil. It also helps to keep the soil in place when the container is lowered into the water.

5 Flood the container with water and let it stand for a while. This reduces the chance of the water becoming muddy when you lower it into the pond.

6 Place the container in a shallow part of the pond initially, especially if new leaves are about to develop. Move it into deeper water a week or two later.

Planning and Planting
SIMPLE SHAPES

Tiny gardens benefit from simple designs, so that they remain uncluttered and any geometric shapes are obvious and easy to see. In this garden it is the choice of plants that will transform it from a simple plan to a striking and well-designed garden with plenty of impact despite its small size. The design pivots around a tiny diamond-shaped lawn, set on the angle of the brick pathway.

PLANNING

It's never a good idea to divide a tiny garden with a straight path from door to gate, which has the effect of slicing it into two smaller pieces, but don't be afraid to keep the design simple. Here, by positioning the gate towards the centre of the boundary it has been possible to introduce a strong line, while varying the depths of the beds allows for more interesting planting. Even so, this arrangement could have still been dull without the extra dimension created by the Corsican mint lawn. This can be used as an intimate sitting area, but its role as a textural feature is equally important.

In the photograph opposite, the plants are still small; after a season or two little of the soil or mulch would be visible.

CHOOSING A NON-GRASS LAWN
Corsican mint and thyme lawns can be planted in the same way – in the photographs opposite, thyme is being used.

PLANTING

HOW TO PLANT NON-LAWN GRASS

1 Thoroughly dig over the area and clear the ground of weeds at least a month before planting. Hoe off any seedlings that appear in the mean time. Rake the ground level before planting.

2 Water the plants in their pots, then set them out about 15–20cm (6–8in) apart, in staggered rows to work out the position and how many plants you need.

3 Knock a plant from its pot and carefully tease out a few of the roots if they are running tightly around the edge of the pot.

4 Plant to the original depth, and firm the soil around the roots before knocking out and planting the next plant. Water thoroughly and keep well watered for the first season.

Planning and Planting
CREATING FOCAL POINTS

Drawing the eye inwards helps to overcome some of the shortcomings of a garden as tiny as this. Focal points like the chimney pot and containers take the eye to individual elements within the design rather than passing straight over the garden from gate to door in a single glance.

PLANNING

reflect the style associated with the period in which the house was built. With a small garden like this, where the house forms a dominant backdrop, it's important that home and garden look well integrated and harmonize as much as possible.

A NEAT EDGE
Emphasize the profile of your beds and borders, as well as your paths, by giving them a crisp or interesting edge. Select an edging that suits the style of your garden. If you prefer an old-fashioned look, reproduction edgings are now readily available.

OTHER IDEAS

Try using empty wine bottles, neck-down, for an unusual edging – leave just a couple of centimetres (an inch) or so of bottle showing.

If you live in a coastal area, consider using large seashells for an edging.

Here containers of various kinds have been used as focal points, and they are especially useful at those times of the year when there is little colour and plants in the borders have died back. Like the previous design, the path has a diversion, which avoids a straight walk from gate to door.

Although modern paving setts have been used for the path, a "rope" edging has been used to

PLANTING

NEAT EDGING

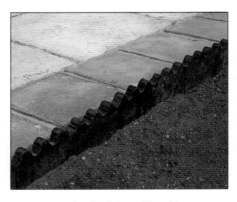

1 For a period garden, Victorian-style rope edging looks appropriate. You can use it to retain a gravel path or as an edging to a paved path.

2 Wavy-edged edgings like this are also reminiscent of some of the older styles of garden, but they can also be used to advantage in a modern setting to give a formal effect.

3 Sawn log rolls make a strong and attractive edging where you want a flowerbed to be raised slightly above a lawn, but remember it may be difficult to mow right up to the edge.

Planning and Planting
NEAT CORNERING

Corner sites can present special problems, but this design has unusually managed to marry straight lines and curves in a successful and distinctive way. It sometimes pays to be bold and imaginative when the site is a difficult one.

PLANNING

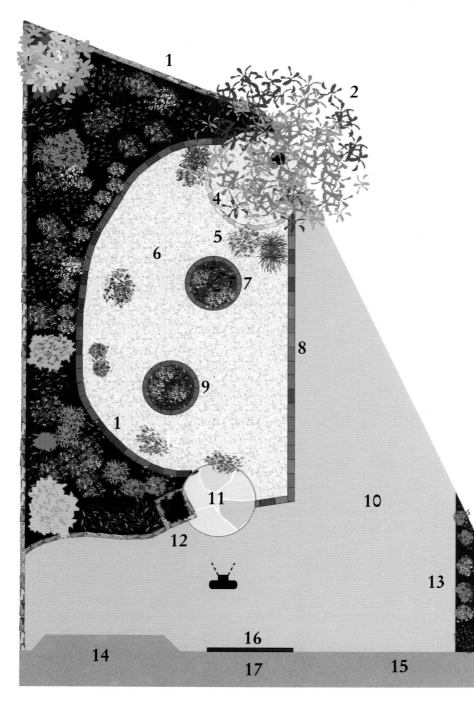

KEY TO PLAN

1 Low wall
2 Birch tree
3 Mixed planting
4 Raised circular bed
5 Plants in gravel
6 Gravel
7 Brick-edged bed with perennials
8 Brick edge
9 Brick-edged bed with seasonal plants
10 Drive
11 Circular stone area
12 Stone pillar with planting area
13 Dwarf shrubs
14 Bay window
15 Garage
16 Door
17 House

Viewpoint on photograph

Awkward corner sites can be especially difficult to design, and if they also have to accommodate a driveway too, the problem is further compounded.

Maximum use has been made of the existing birch tree in this plan, as it takes the eye from the bleakness of the drive. Creating a circular bed around it emphasizes it as a focal point, and to give the garden a sense of unity, the circular theme has been repeated with a couple of round raised beds and an interesting circular stone feature, linking the drive and gravel area.

USING GRAVEL
Gravel is best laid over a weed-suppressing base, but it's still possible to plant through both materials if necessary.

PLANTING

HOW TO LAY AND PLANT THROUGH GRAVEL

1 Dig the area to hold 5cm (2in) of gravel. Level the ground, then lay heavy-duty black plastic or a mulching sheet over the area. Overlap strips by about 5cm (2in).

2 Tip gravel on to the sheet, then rake it level. To plant through the gravel, draw back an area of gravel from where you plan to plant and make a slit in the plastic.

3 Plant normally through the slit, enriching the soil beneath if necessary with fertilizer or garden compost.

4 Firm in the plant with your hand and water thoroughly, then smooth the plastic back and re-cover the area with gravel.

Choosing Plants
PLANTS FOR SMALL GARDENS

Almost any plant other than medium-sized or tall trees or very large shrubs and rampant ground cover can be grown in a small garden. Often quite large plants are used, but they need to be pruned back regularly to maintain a compact size. Whenever possible, it's best to choose naturally compact plants that won't become a nuisance.

EVERGREEN TREES

If conifers are excluded, there are few evergreen trees suitable for a small garden. Few broad-leaved trees are evergreen in temperate climates, and unfortunately many of those that are, such as the evergreen oak (*Quercus ilex*), grow far too large for most gardens. There are some worth searching out, such as *Drimys winteri*, which is too large for a tiny garden, but is not a fast grower. It's not a good choice for cold areas, however. Hollies (ilex) are really tough, and can be trained into a conical or standard tree with a clear trunk.

Drimys winteri is an uncommon plant, especially where winters are cold, but it makes an interesting large shrub or small tree with large, leathery evergreen leaves and fragrant white flowers in late spring.

DECIDUOUS TREES

It's a pity to exclude trees from a small garden, but choose those that remain small and have more than one season of interest. *Acer griseum*, for example, has a lovely cinnamon bark which looks

Crataegus oxyacantha (now more correctly *C. laevigata*) 'Rosea Flore Pleno' is a pretty hawthorn with double pink flowers in late spring. These trees never become very large.

wonderful in winter sunlight as well as fantastic in autumn colour. Many hawthorns (crataegus) make pleasing compact trees for a small garden. For flowering trees, look for those with columnar growth, such as *Prunus* 'Amanogawa'.

CONIFERS

Conifers come in many shades of gold and green (some with a hint of blue), as well as various shapes and sizes. The vast majority are evergreen. Unfortunately, most of them grow far too tall for a small garden. Select those with narrow, columnar growth that will not ultimately become too tall. Some to look for are *Juniperus scopulorum* 'Skyrocket', *Juniperus communis* 'Hibernica' and *Taxus baccata* 'Fastigiata Aurea'. *Cupressus macrocarpa* 'Goldcrest' also has a pleasing upright profile as well as a bright colour.

DWARF CONIFERS

A visit to any garden centre will reveal a bewildering choice of dwarf conifers, but always check on likely size after say 10 or 15 years of growth. Some will remain dwarf and may even be at home in

Cupressus macrocarpa 'Goldcrest' eventually makes a medium-sized tree, but has a narrow growth that means it does not take up excessive ground space. Young foliage is a beautiful yellow

a rock garden; others may grow surprisingly large. Among those that grow shrub-size are *Thuja orientalis* 'Aurea Nana', *Thuja occidentalis* 'Rheingold' and *Chamaecyparis pisifera* 'Filifera Aurea'. *Juniperus squamata* 'Blue Star' remains low-growing, and there are many other ground-hugging conifers.

EVERGREEN SHRUBS

You will be spoilt for choice with evergreen shrubs, so decide how large or small you want the plant

Thuja occidentalis 'Rheingold' is slow-growing and forms an oval to conical bush that always looks neat. The colour is old gold, and is especially pleasing in winter.

to grow to reduce your short list. If you have an acid soil, rhododendrons are a likely choice, but some can grow huge while others are suitable for a rock garden. There are bound to be varieties of appropriate size for your needs. Hebes are also available in many shapes and sizes, but always check that the ones you like are winter-hardy in your area. Heathers are evergreen and they are bound to be compact enough for your garden. The winter-flowering *Erica carnea* varieties are especially useful.

Hebe x *franciscana* 'Variegata' is delightfully bright and compact dwarf shrub, but it may suffer – or even be killed – where winters are cold.

DECIDUOUS SHRUBS

The problem with many deciduous shrubs is their short period of interest: flowering sometimes lasting no more than a couple of weeks. To make the best use of space, choose some that have golden or variegated foliage for a longer period of interest, or select those that have early colour, like chaenomeles, which bloom in spring, or that have late-season interest, like *Cotoneaster horizontalis* with its bright berries and vivid autumn foliage colour. Some, such as hydrangeas, also retain their flowers for a long period, and the dead heads also make an interesting winter feature.

The flower colour of *Hydrangea macrophylla* is often affected by the acidity or alkalinity of the soil.

BORDER PLANTS

All but the largest and tallest or most rampant herbaceous plants are suitable for a small garden, but where space is limited it's best to concentrate on those that flower early or late, or that look good over a long period and don't only look good for a week or two in summer. Lupins look fantastic for a couple of weeks, but for the rest of the season offer little interest.

Doronicums have nothing to offer by the time summer arrives, but they make an eye-catching display in spring.

Select summer flowers that bloom over a long period, or that have attractive foliage. For early border flowers, doronicums, with their yellow daisy-type flowers, look good, while at the end of the season schizostylis and varieties and hybrids of *Sedum spectabile* will sustain the colour.

EVERGREEN BORDER PLANTS

Make a point of visiting gardens in winter, and note which border plants remain evergreen. There are not many of them, but they are invaluable for sustaining interest during the bleak months. They include bergenias, ajugas and *Stachys byzantina*.

Ajuga reptans 'Atropurpurea' is one of several attractive bugles that make an attractive edging. They are almost evergreen and grow in sun and shade.

FAMILY GARDENS

Some gardens are designed primarily to be admired, others to be lived in –
a place where children can play and adults can relax and perhaps enjoy a meal
with friends. With careful thought, however, it's possible to design a garden
that's both good to look at and comfortable to live in.

Children make the most demands on a garden, not least because they require
a play area, which may not always be compatible with the kind of flower
garden you have in mind, but also because the plants near play areas have to
be that much tougher to withstand the occasional ball or rowdy play. It's a
good idea to ban thorny or prickly plants, such as roses, in this area, to
avoid unnecessary injuries.

Where there are very small children, ponds are not a good idea unless they
are well protected. Some people fence them off or install protective metal
covers for them, but such devices will not enhance the visual appeal of your
pond and can be decidedly off-putting. It may be better to choose a water
feature without standing water while the children are young.

■ ABOVE
Somewhere to entertain and relax is an essential ingredient of a family garden.

■ OPPOSITE
A place for the family to play and a desirable garden don't have to be an
impossible mix. Turn a swing into a feature, rather than hiding it away.

INSPIRATIONAL IDEAS

Children can enjoy "adult" gardens, too, especially if there are lots of interesting shrubs and plants. Plants with big or bold leaves, or insectivorous plants, will stimulate their imagination and encourage interest as they grow older.

■ BELOW
A play area can be incorporated into the garden plan as easily as any other feature. Here, the sandpit has been positioned between two wooden walkways, with another small play area beyond the flowerbed. Using the small bed to divide up the play zone like this ensures it forms part of the garden and is not perceived as an appendage divorced from the garden proper.

■ **ABOVE**
Children would love this walkway along
the back of a border and the climbing
mesh against the other wall. And when
they have outgrown such fun things,
they can be removed, and the garden is
left without any redesigning to be done.

■ **RIGHT**
This is unashamedly a garden for grown-
ups to enjoy in the evening, but children
will be fascinated by its magical grotto-
like enchantment.

   Illuminating part of your garden will
enable you to derive many more hours
of pleasure from it, and it will be a
marvellous place to entertain your
friends on a summer evening.

INSPIRATIONAL IDEAS

It is possible to create a stylish design that will appeal to parents and children in equal measure. A well-designed garden should be flexible enough to accommodate a safe play area for children and an entertainment and dining area for the whole family to enjoy.

■ ABOVE
Older children, able to use a trampoline unattended for example, do not usually have to be supervised so closely. As equipment like this is not an attractive feature in design terms, it's best to tuck it away out of sight, but not on a hard paved surface. This one has been positioned in a large bay of the lawn screened from the house by shrub borders.

■ OPPOSITE
A lawn for play is an essential part of a garden that young children can enjoy, but it can be a challenge to accommodate larger toys such as swings or see-saws. In this garden, the swing has been positioned in an area of the lawn that is clearly visible for supervision, but an "adult" space can easily be reinstated when the swing is no longer required.

Know-how
EATING OUT

Family gardens have to be multi-purpose, but, unless the garden is large, it may be necessary to place the design emphasis on one or two particular needs. If you do lots of entertaining, then a barbecue and seating area is likely to be a priority; if you seldom ask people around for outdoor meals but have young children who need somewhere safe and secure to play, a lawn and play area may be more important to you.

Eating out in the garden is so much more relaxing than meals around the dining table. Children love the fun of a barbecue, but there's a lot to be said for the convenience of preparing the food indoors and simply taking it outside to eat. A barbecue can be a colourful and cheerful occasion, and a time when your labours in the garden will be appreciated by all the family.

■ BELOW
ADDING COLOUR A bright or colourful tablecloth will transform a drab table in an instant. Add a few pots of seasonal plants, or a simple flower arrangement, for that finishing touch.
DESIGN TIP *Be prepared to move the table around the garden on different occasions, to take advantage of seasonal plants. Use a variety of bright tablecloths to keep each occasion special.*

GARDEN LIGHTS Even the simplest meal becomes an adventure for children if it's eaten outdoors after dark. Patio lights that you can fix to a sunshade are simple to install and provide all the light you need for a simple occasion like this.

DESIGN TIP *Garden lights can transform your garden after dusk, but be careful with the use of spotlights – wherever possible make sure they point down rather than up if there is a risk of their shining into your neighbour's house. Patio lights cast a glow rather than a strong beam so should not be annoying to neighbours, and the parasol helps to confine the light and cast it downwards.*

■ ABOVE

KEEP IT SIMPLE A few flowers and foliage picked from the garden, a simple salad seasoned with fresh herbs and a bowl of strawberries, will provide all the ingredients for a relaxing meal in the garden. For a quick meal, keep it simple: you'll enjoy it as much as something more lavish in this relaxing environment.

DESIGN TIP *Don't be content with a natural wood finish. Be prepared to paint the table and chairs if this creates an interesting focal point, or helps to express your creative sense of design.*

■ RIGHT

PORTABLE TABLES This small garden has all the essential elements for outdoor living: a built-in barbecue, a pretty setting and a bottle of wine at the ready. You don't need to set aside a large area for this kind of outdoor living.

DESIGN TIP *If the garden or sitting area is very small, a lightweight and easily portable table that can be brought out for the occasion might make better use of the available space than heavy, fixed or less mobile furniture.*

Know-how
SITTING PRETTY

Seating is an integral part of most gardens, but in a family garden it can be used to suggest a place for everyone – children and parents – to sit and enjoy the pleasures that outdoor living and a well-planned garden can bring.

■ **RIGHT**
DESIGNING WITH CHAIRS A seat that has its own space built into the design will always make the garden look well planned and structured.
DESIGN TIP *It's important to have the exact seat in mind at the design stage, as the recess must look made-to-measure.*

■ **BELOW**
BENCH SEATS Children will probably be as happy sitting on a seat made from old railway sleepers (railroad ties) as on stylish manufactured furniture.
DESIGN TIP *A seat like this is best positioned in an informal part of the garden, perhaps near or among trees, where it will blend in with the background and look more sympathetic with the surroundings than more traditional seats.*

■ LEFT

FEATURE SEATS Improvised seats can be a test of initiative, but are great fun to make. Children will find them exciting to sit on, and they often make decorative focal points. This one is made from an old garden roller, with a clipped dwarf hedge for the surround.

DESIGN TIP *Try to position a seat like this where it also makes a focal point when viewed across the garden.*

■ RIGHT

USING TREES Tree seats always attract admiring comments, and they appeal to children as much as parents. A seat like this can make a feature in an area of the garden that might otherwise lack interest. White paint helps to bring light to what can be a gloomy position, and attracts the eye from across the garden.

DESIGN TIP *Choose a tree with a large trunk, if possible. If you build a seat around a fairly slim tree, the proportions will look wrong and the impact will be less effective.*

Know-how

A Relaxing Time

Family gardens should look lived-in, and loungers and hammocks will create this relaxed and friendly atmosphere. There are many types to choose from – select seating that will match the style of your garden, whether it be formal or country cottage.

■ **LEFT**
HAMMOCK If you have a stately tree, it can become a support for a hammock and a swing seat for the children or grandchildren. A corner of the garden like this can be shared by all generations of the family.
DESIGN TIP *A shady tree is the best location for a hammock.*

■ **BELOW**
SUN LOUNGERS Loungers can be moved around the garden with ease. If you choose a bold colour, they will act as a focal point.
DESIGN TIP *Placing two or more loungers together gives the impression of shared pleasure. Placing a small table between them with a collection of cool drinks will look even more tempting.*

■ LEFT
WOODEN FURNITURE
Even wooden garden furniture can be made comfortable with a few cushions, and a feature like this can be easily incorporated into almost any plan.
DESIGN TIP
Wherever possible, position your furniture as near as you can to fragrant plants.

■ RIGHT
POOLSIDE LOUNGERS
Sometimes a quiet place to lounge in tranquil isolation, perhaps to read a book or have a nap, is more appealing than a spot on a sunny lawn with the rest of the family.
DESIGN TIP
A simple piece of garden furniture like this pool lounger can serve as a useful focal point in an otherwise flat area.

Know-how
SOMEWHERE TO PLAY

Children love their own play area and will especially enjoy a play house, or even a tree house if they are old enough. It's their part of the garden, and the chances are that, by keeping most of their rough-and-tumble activity in one place, the rest of the garden will remain looking smart and beautiful.

■ **RIGHT**
ASSAULT COURSE These steps up to a platform take children to an exciting assault-course slide. This is less ambitious than a tree house, but potentially as much fun for children.

■ **BELOW**
ADVENTURE PLAYGROUND If you have a large garden, you have the potential for a small adventure playground. These climbing frames, made from rustic poles, blend happily into the garden. Chipped bark has been spread over the ground to soften any falls and prevent slippery, muddy areas. Always make sure such structures are absolutely stable.

■ **LEFT**
WENDY HOUSE This delightful little crooked house, complete with veranda and cute chimney, has been built on stilts with a short stairway leading up to it. It is a dream house for a child with imagination. Always make sure elevated structures are absolutely safe, and take advice from a builder if in doubt.

■ **BELOW**
PLAY HOUSE A play house is a young child's delight, and it may be possible to accommodate one at an end of the patio so that supervision is possible, when required. It doesn't have to be left in the original wood finish. Painting it an attractive colour may transform it into a desirable garden feature, and the children will love it, especially if consulted about the colour.

Planning and Planting
URBAN ELEGANCE

This town garden is the perfect place to relax in, to unwind from the stresses of a busy life. The dominance of greens and whites in the planting plan gives the garden a sense of unity and subtlety, as well as a sense of cool tranquillity.

PLANNING

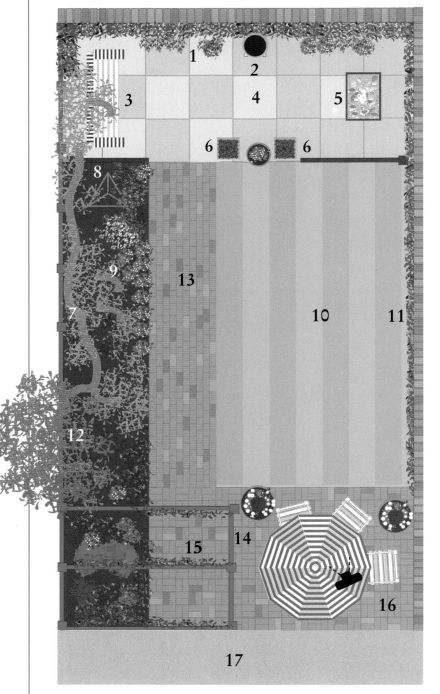

KEY TO PLAN

1 Hedge
2 Urn
3 Garden swing seat
4 Paved area
5 Pebble fountain
6 Clipped box
7 Trellis
8 Tripod for climbers
9 Low raised bed with mixed planting
10 Lawn
11 Wall climbers
12 Specimen tree, pruned and trained to grow along boundary
13 Brick path
14 Patio overhead (beams above window level)
15 Climber over patio overhead
16 Patio
17 House
✿ Viewpoint on photograph

This is primarily the kind of garden that would appeal to adults, but there is a large lawn for anyone who needs to let off steam. However, a high-quality lawn like this is too good for rough play: a paved area is more suitable for ball games or frequent use. The lawn is an important and dominant design features of this plan, creating a sense of open space that lets the garden "breathe".

The tree on the left-hand side of the garden is unusual as it has been persuaded to grow along the edge of the garden rather than over it, so avoiding a potential shade problem. A small tree, left to grow naturally, would be just as effective in this situation.

As planting space is limited, the bed along the side of the garden accommodates seasonal plants and permanent evergreen plants, to pack in colour where it's needed, and to introduce an element of variety from season to season.

■ RIGHT

HOW TO BUILD PATIO OVERHEADS

Patio overheads are a kind of pergola with one end of the overhead beams fixed to the house or garden wall. These are particularly effective for linking the home and garden visually, and of course they provide a useful support for climbers as well as a degree of shade. If you want a more enclosed structure, with permanent shading and a greater degree of privacy, it's possible to fix reed mats over the top, although

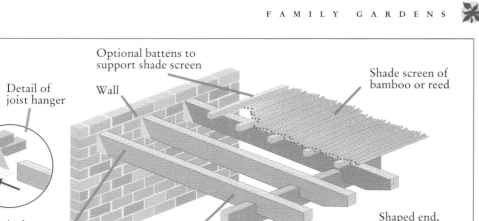

Detail of joist hanger

Wall

Optional battens to support shade screen

Shade screen of bamboo or reed

Joist hanger mortared between brick courses

Floor joists used as beams

Shaped end, to make it more attractive and reduce weight

PLANNING

additional battens, laid at right angles to the overhead beams, will be required to support them.

Remember that patio overheads that join the house should always be high enough to clear the window and not block out the view if vigorous climbers cascade from the beams.

Use floor joists for the overhead beams, and secure them to the wall with joist hangers (see illustration). These are designed with a lip to be mortared into the brickwork, so on an existing wall it will be necessary to chisel out sufficient mortar to accommodate the hanger. Once the joist hanger has been mortared into position and the mortar has set, the beam can be inserted and secured by nailing through the fixing holes in the hanger. The hangers are available from builders' merchants and large do-it-yourself stores.

If the span is short, the beams may only require the support of one cross-beam supported on posts, as shown. Wider spans will need intermediate post and beam supports.

If you wish to add shading for summer, nail battens parallel to the wall to support a reed or bamboo screen (these usually come in rolls), as shown in the illustration. If you wish to have the shading in position only for the summer, it should be possible to tie it in position, but do this securely.

Be sure that the posts are strong enough for the structure and that they are well concreted into the ground or fixed in special post supports.

Planning and Planting
A HOUSE OF THEIR OWN

Children's needs often have to be accommodated within an existing garden, or designed into a new one in a way that, when the facilities have been outgrown, they can be removed without leaving an obtrusive space or in need of re-designing. Here, the children's area has been created in a part of the garden separate from the main ornamental area.

PLANNING

An area for children should reflect their ages, and of course with a growing family there may be a spread of ages to accommodate, all needing different kinds of stimulation. This plan shows features that will appeal to young children and older ones.

In a garden like this, younger children will have to be supervised carefully, for there are hard surfaces. Thorny plants like roses are a potential hazard, and a tree house will definitely be out of bounds for the very young. Older children will love the tree house and the den, however, and a garden with hiding places and secret corners will feed their imagination.

Depending on the age of the youngest child, it may be necessary to fence off the area beyond the play house, with a gate to the adventure area beyond.

PLAY HOUSES
You should be able to add a few finishing touches to the basic structure of a store-bought, manufactured play house, and if your children are involved in choosing the embellishments and colour schemes, they'll find it that much more exciting.

PLANTING

HOW TO CUSTOMIZE A PLAY HOUSE

1 The original play house had a simple wood finish, treated against rot but not particularly attractive.

2 The play house has been transformed by the addition of shuttered windows and mineral-fibre roof slates and, of course, a coat of paint. You could use gloss paint, a coloured woodstain or coloured preservative.

3 Small ridge tiles and a decorative fascia complete the transformation, along with a hanging basket.

Planning and Planting
OUTDOOR ENTERTAINING

This garden is clearly designed for the whole family to enjoy the great outdoors in the garden. There are plenty of seats for family and friends, a built-in barbecue, and a sand pit for youngsters. There's also plenty of space to play in this safe and enclosed environment.

PLANNING

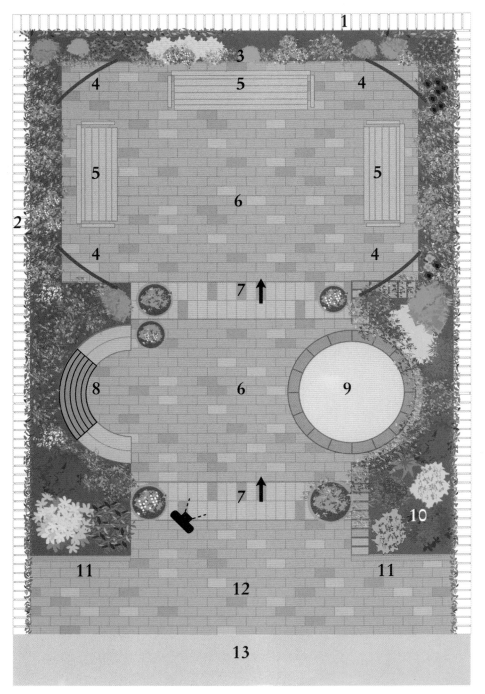

This garden shows many design elements that guarantee impact: changes of level, a choice of areas for sitting and relaxing, attractive paving that harmonizes with the walls, some strong focal points, and a symmetry of construction that suggests good design.

It may seem strange that a sandpit should become a focal point, but when its usefulness as a sandpit is over, and young children have grown up, it can be turned into an attractive circular pond, perhaps with a fountain to bring movement and relaxing sounds to the scene.

LIGHTING UP
Garden lighting can be enchanting and atmospheric, and it can even make your garden a safer place if potentially hazardous steps are illuminated. If you are considering installing a high-voltage system, you should always consult a qualified electrician. A low-voltage system, however, is a relatively simple do-it-yourself job, but take professional advice, if in doubt.

PLANTING

GARDEN LIGHTING

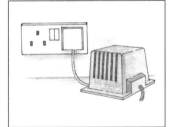  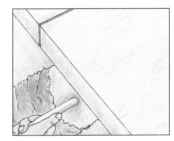 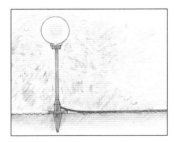

1 A low-voltage lighting kit will come with a transformer. This must always be protected from the weather, positioned in a dry place indoors or in a garage or outbuilding.

2 Using an electric drill, make a hole through the window frame or wall, just wide enough to take the cable. Fill in any gaps afterwards, using a mastic or other waterproof filler.

3 Although the cable carries a low voltage, it is still a potential hazard if left uncovered. Unless the lights are positioned close to where the cable emerges, run it underground in a conduit.

4 Most low-voltage lighting systems are designed to be moved around. Many of them can be pushed conveniently into the ground wherever you choose to use them.

Planning and Planting
LINE AND COLOUR

The planting in this garden is secondary to the impact of strong lines and colours, and it is clearly designed primarily as an outdoor room for eating and entertainment.

PLANNING

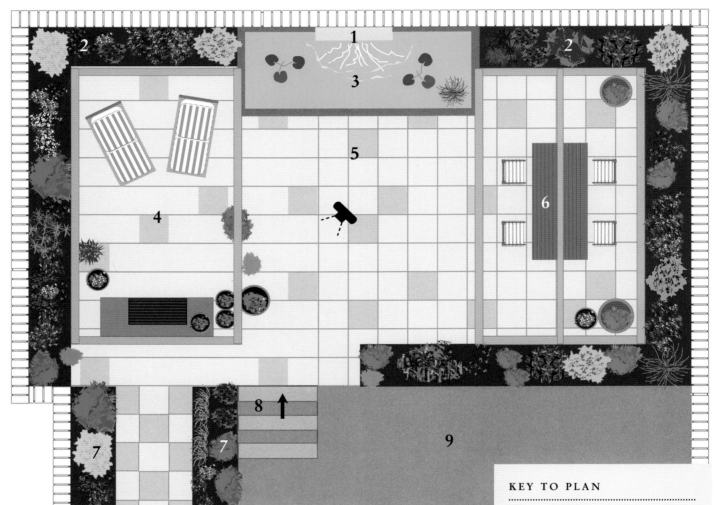

Many garden designs place the emphasis on plants, but if your interests lie in relaxation and outdoor living rather than in gardening as a hobby, it's a good idea to confine the planting to a few beds as a backdrop or to soften the harsh effect of walls or fences. A garden like this, designed for lots of outdoor eating and entertaining, may be used much more intensively for relaxation than designs intended primarily to show off the plants.

SUN SHADES
Sunny summer days are what we all dream of, but there are times when we all need to retreat to some shade. Parasols and awnings can be pretty as well as practical, and they can make striking focal points.

KEY TO PLAN

1 Wall fountain
2 Low-growing mixed plants
3 Pond
4 Barbecue and relaxing area
5 Tile paving
6 Eating area with patio overhead
7 Low-growing shrubs
8 Steps
9 House

↑ Direction of steps down

🔦 Viewpoint on photograph

■ ABOVE
Parasols like this can have as much impact as a flowerbed, and they make stylish focal points.

PLANTING

■ ABOVE
MIDDLE
An awning is a useful windbreak for a breezy day as well as a practical sunshade for when you need to retreat to somewhere cool. This one comes with a lightweight metal frame that is easily erected, and the awning is simply slipped over it.

■ ABOVE RIGHT
You couldn't help but feel grand sheltering from the blistering sun in this elegant structure, which would bring colour to your garden even if the flowers were not performing. A teepee structure like this helps to create a feeling of cosy intimacy as you share a meal beneath it.

Planning and Planting

AN ENCHANTED JUNGLE

This dense, lush garden has both sophistication for grown-ups and drama and adventure for children, with changes of level and lots of tall, leafy plants, including a banana plant, bedded out for the summer. This plan is perfect for dining and playing.

PLANNING

KEY TO PLAN

1 Shrubs
2 Decking with table and chairs
3 Decking at higher level
4 Steps
5 A focal-point foliage plant (here a banana plant)
6 Barbecue
7 Group of containers
8 Patio
9 Door
10 House

↓ Direction of steps down

Viewpoint on photograph

Even a small area can look densely planted if you envelop your sitting area with a living screen of well-chosen plants. Changing levels and using shrubs to obscure the various sections of the garden also help to make it an exciting garden to explore and play in.

The choice of decking in this design helps to create a jungle-like atmosphere as it blends in perfectly with the plants, having a natural affinity with them.

The lower paved area acts as a practical bridge between home and the plant-filled area, and it is here that the barbecue has been situated, leaving the eating area free of anything that would detract from its natural-looking setting.

GIANT FOLIAGE PLANTS
An impressive banana plant has been used as a focal-point foliage plant in the garden photographed opposite, but such exotic plants need to be over-wintered in a conservatory or a large greenhouse if you live where temperatures drop to freezing. There are many hardy foliage plants with big or

PLANNING

bold leaves, however, and a clump of them can create the impression of lush, tropical growth.

The plants in the illustration all prefer moist soil, such as that found in a bog garden, but you can grow them in a normal bed or border if you use a trickle irrigation hose to ensure adequate moisture. Where conditions suit, the gunnera leaves can grow to 1.8m (6ft) across on stems up to 3m (10ft) tall, though in dry conditions they will be probably be smaller.

GIANT FOLIAGE PLANTS

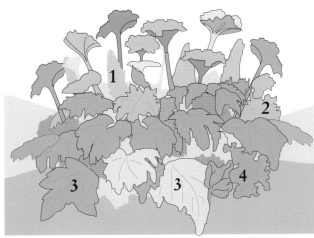

KEY TO PLANTS

1 *Gunnera manicata*
2 *Petasites japonicus giganteus*
3 *Rheum undulatum*
4 *Rheum palmatum tanguticum*

Planning and Planting

A SECRET GARDEN

This garden has lots of features packed into a modest-sized plot, happily marrying an open area of lawn for relaxation and play with plenty of screening and a sense of seclusion.

PLANNING

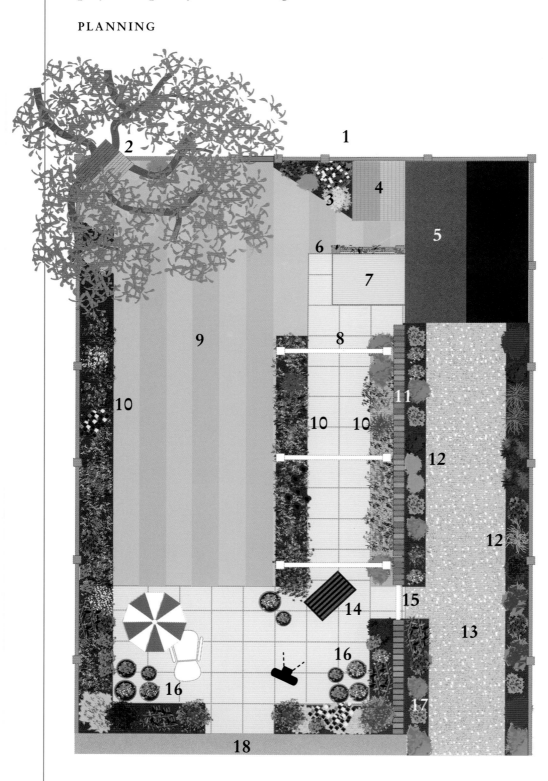

Children have been well catered for in this garden, with a sandpit and a tree house, together with a lawn where the whole family can play and relax. The pergola gives shade and a sense of seclusion, and it ensures that the garden has height and a sense of structure. A trellis positioned behind the sandpit helps to screen the garden shed from view.

A garage and drive can dominate a garden if not screened. Here a dividing wall solves the problem by disguising the drive. If building a brick wall seems a daunting job, screen (pierced) walling blocks are easy to lay and will still act as a screen, especially if climbers or shrubs are used to clothe them.

LIGHTWEIGHT PERGOLAS
The strongest pergolas are made from sawn wood (lumber), but a lightweight structure can be easily constructed from rustic poles and will blend in with the surroundings effectively.

PLANTING

HOW TO JOIN RUSTIC POLES

1 Using a handsaw, saw a notch of suitable size at the top of the upright post to take a horizontal piece of wood snugly.

2 Where two rails have to be joined, do this over an upright. Cut matching notches so that one piece sits directly over the other.

3 To fix crosspieces to horizontals, cut a V-shaped notch into the crosspiece, using a chisel if necessary, then nail into place.

4 Use halving joints where two pieces cross. Make two saw cuts halfway through the pole, then chisel out the waste. Use a wood adhesive and secure a halving joint with a nail for extra strength.

5 Bird's-mouth joints are useful for connecting horizontal and diagonal pieces to uprights. Remove a V-shaped notch about 2.5cm (1in) deep, then saw the other piece to match. Use a chisel to achieve a good fit.

Choosing Plants
PLANTS FOR FAMILY GARDENS

Most plants have a place in the family garden, and the best plants are simply those that you like, provided they are not harmful. It is easier to suggest plants to avoid rather than specific plants to grow. However, plants with large, unusual or dramatic foliage will be popular.

PLANTS TO AVOID

Avoid very spiky plants, but take care: the leaf tips of Spanish bayonet (*Yucca gloriosa*) look no more hazardous than other yuccas, but this one has treacherous leaf tips that arch out and can cause a painful stab. Roses with many or large thorns are also best avoided.

Potentially poisonous or irritant plants should also be avoided. Some have poisonous roots or leaves, but berries are the greatest hazard as they look tempting. Some plants cause dermatitis and other skin irritations. A few are potentially very hazardous, however, a common one being rue (*Ruta graveolens*), the sap of which can cause a very severe allergic reaction on bare skin in sunlight.

FASCINATING ARUMS

Aroids, plants of the arum family, are strange plants that children will find fascinating. The arum lily

Dracunculus vulgaris is not a plant you could pass by without noticing – at least not when it is in full flower. Their eye-catching crimson flowers have a very unpleasant smell.

(*Zantedeschia aethiopica*) is often grown as a cut flower and as a pot plant in conservatories, but where winters are not severe it can be grown as a garden plant, too. Arums have their true flowers clustered inconspicuously on a club-like or poker-shaped spadix, which is surrounded by the showy coloured spath. For children, try the mouse plant (*Arisarum proboscideum*) or the voodoo lily (*Sauromatum venosum*). The latter can be flowered out of soil or water indoors, then planted in the garden to produce its impressive foliage. The smell of the flowers can literally make you want to vomit, something children can find amusing. For the garden try the dragon arum (*Dracunculus vulgaris*), which has huge velvety-crimson spathes 30–60cm (1–2ft) long and flowers that smell of rotting meat, which attract flies. Other arums have flowers that look like cobra heads.

QUICK AND EASY ANNUALS

Plants that grow quickly, especially from seed to flower in a matter of months, are more likely to hold the interest of youngsters. Small-growers like the poached-egg plant (*Limnanthes douglasii*) are easy for a child to sow and flower, and are worth growing as good garden plants anyway. But it's the tall sunflowers that will probably encourage children to get involved in regular watering and feeding.

Limnanthes douglasii, sometimes known as the poached-egg plant, is a really easy hardy annual to grow. Although the parent plant dies at the end of the season, self-sown seedlings usually appear.

FRUITS FOR FUN

Things that can be safely eaten hold their own special attraction, and apples and pears can make decorative garden features if grown as a cordon or espalier against the garden fence or up a wall. A family apple tree, with several different varieties grafted on to the same plant, is sure to create interest and is an ideal way of growing several varieties in the space of one.

Pears trained as espaliers can, with patience, look much more attractive than those grown in tree form. The fruit will also be very much easier to reach when it comes to harvesting.

BORDER PLANTS

It's a good idea to concentrate on those almost indestructible herbaceous perennials such as day lilies (hemerocallis), red-hot-pokers (kniphofias) and hostas. If you have young children, it may be best to avoid plants that attract bees, such as catmints (nepetas).

Hemerocallis are sometimes called day lilies because individual blooms are so short-lived. Fortunately, a succession of them is produced over a long period.

SHRUBS

For backbone planting, tough variegated evergreens that stand up to occasional rough play yet still

Aucuba japonica 'Variegata' is a really tough shrub, for sun or shade, and a useful evergreen for those difficult spots that every garden has. There are other variegated varieties to choose from.

look good through the year are difficult to beat. You will also need plenty of deciduous flowering shrubs, but as core plants, use shrubs such as *Aucuba japonica* in one of it many variegated forms, *Elaeagnus pungens* 'Maculata' and phormiums (these may be vulnerable where winters are cold).

Elaeagnus pungens 'Maculata' is an outstanding evergreen that looks especially good positioned where winter sunshine can highlight the gold in the variegated leaves.

HERBS

Many of us grow a few herbs for the kitchen, but some of the more interesting ones can get children interested in the different aromas as well as possibly their use at table. A collection of mints with all their various smells, from spearmint to apple, thymes and the tall, aniseed-flavoured fennel (*Foeniculum vulgare*) are good multi-purpose herbs to start with. Herbs in containers, or grown in a herb "wheel" will also keep children involved.

Fennel *(Foeniculum vulgare)* has feathery foliage that makes it an attractive ornamental as well as a culinary herb. There is a bronze form as well as the more common green one.

BULBS

Children enjoy planting bulbs and corms, from which some of our best and brightest flowers come. Get them to plant spring crocuses and autumn-flowering colchicums in borders or a corner of the lawn if it's suitable. Colchicums are especially rewarding as they can flower within weeks of planting. Choose big and spectacular plants for summer bulbs, such as *Allium giganteum* or one of the foxtail lilies (eremurus).

Colchicum autumnale is sometimes called an autumn crocus. Colchicums usually bloom in early autumn, when colour in the garden is becoming scarce.

KITCHEN GARDENS

While some gardeners are uninspired by the concept of kitchen gardens, others are happy to devote much of their free time and all available space to growing vegetables and fruit. Most of us, however, would probably prefer to combine the edible with the ornamental, whether they grow side by side as in a potager or in separate parts of the garden.

It's unreasonable to expect self-sufficiency in produce from all but the largest gardens, and even then few are prepared to devote the time and effort required. Most of us aspire to be good gardeners, not smallholders, so the ability to harvest our own new potatoes while they are still expensive in the shops, pick an apple from the tree and take a bite, or perhaps have a constant supply of salad crops and herbs during the summer, is all we ask. It is the satisfaction of having grown your own, and the knowledge that they are fresh and free from pesticides (assuming you've been careful on this point), that's the special reward.

■ ABOVE
Every garden has space for fruits and vegetables, and the benefits are great.

■ OPPOSITE
Red cabbages, contained by a dwarf box (*Buxus sempervirens* 'Suffruticosa') hedge, look highly ornamental.

INSPIRATIONAL IDEAS

Growing plants that you can eat as well as admire is a bonus. Some vegetables, such as ruby chard and beetroot, even cut-leaved lettuce, are pretty as ornamental plants in beds and borders. Try planting vegetables and fruit in beds and borders, with flowers.

■ BELOW

A kitchen garden is likely to be visually more acceptable if it is broken up into small beds, here with a decorative "rope" edging. The crops are easy to cultivate without having to walk on the soil, as all parts can be reached with a hoe from the paths. It's possible to arrange the beds in a geometrical pattern to emphasize the sense of design. The paths between them can also be made interesting, depending on the materials used and how they are laid. Here light-coloured bricks complement the rope edging, unifying the design.

■ OPPOSITE ABOVE

In a cottage garden, it's perfectly natural to see a corner given over to growing vegetables. Provided it is a weed-free and neat area, it should not look unattractive. Adding a few bright flowers around the edge, like these French marigolds, will make it look more ornamental – and it is thought that these plants can help to deter pests.

■ OPPOSITE BELOW

Old-fashioned cottage gardens often used to have vegetables in the front garden, and crops like pumpkins and squashes were very decorative towards the end of the season. Don't be afraid to use a few flowers alongside the vegetables. This practice used to be quite common and, as this picture shows, makes a far more pleasing garden than vegetables alone. The white picket fence also makes this a lively garden to look at and shows that the kitchen garden does not have to be tucked away in a utilitarian part of the entire garden.

INSPIRATIONAL IDEAS

You don't need space for an orchard to grow your own fruit. Apples, pears and peaches are among the fruits easily trained against a wall or fence as a fan, espalier or cordon. Soft fruit such as strawberries can be grown in pots or in small beds in sunny positions.

■ OPPOSITE

Herb gardens are sometimes created more for their ornamental effect than for culinary benefits. There's lots of scope for geometric designs, and focal-point features such as birdbaths and sundials.

■ RIGHT

If you garden on a patio or balcony, your herbs may have to be confined to containers. This is not always a bad thing: the mints in this growing bag will remain confined and the spreading roots will not be able to invade surrounding territory. Next to the mints is a collection of three attractive ornamental sages, and the remaining pot holds a small collection of various herbs.

These practical herbs have been placed unashamedly against a raised bed with flowers as a backdrop: petunias and the yellow trailing *Lysimachia nummularia*.

■ ABOVE

Kitchen gardens can make charming decorative features. In this walled garden, the design has been marked out by edgings of box or rue, but the contents of each bed are surprisingly diverse. Some contain potatoes or tomatoes, in others ornamental plants such as dahlias are growing.

There are also beds with herbs, and beds containing soft fruits such as gooseberries.

Despite the diversity of plants being grown within the beds – vegetables, herbs, fruit, and flowers – the design looks unified and well planned because the area has been laid out to a recognizable pattern.

Know-how
KITCHEN CONTAINERS

If you don't have space for a large kitchen garden, think creatively. It may be possible to grow a small selection that combines the ornamental with the tasty.

Salad crops such as tomatoes and lettuces are especially good for growing in containers, as they respond well to confinement, they are easy to grow, and you don't need many plants for a small family. They can be grown in window boxes or patio pots. Be prepared to stretch your horizons, however, as most vegetables can be grown successfully in containers with a little determination.

■ BELOW LEFT
LETTUCES Lettuces are really easy to grow, and small varieties don't require much space. Sow a pinch of seeds each week from spring onwards for a succession of hearted lettuce, or choose loose-leaf types such as 'Salad Bowl' so that you can harvest individual leaves over a long period. This does not leave such obvious gaps when you harvest, in comparison with a hearty variety where you use the whole head.

Choose different types of lettuce with a variety of leaf shape and colour, to make attractive displays in troughs, containers or window boxes.

DESIGN TIP *If growing in window boxes, use two or three liner boxes (cheap plastic troughs) to fit inside a more attractive outer box. Sow in succession in the various boxes, and move those at their most attractive stage into the decorative outer box. When harvesting is over, replace the inner trough with one containing maturing lettuces and resow the one removed.*

■ RIGHT
POTATOES Maincrop potatoes are not a practical proposition for containers, but it's worth planting a few tubers of an early variety to bring on and harvest while the tubers are still small and especially tasty. This is the time when potatoes are also at their most expensive in the shops. Start them off in a frost-free greenhouse or conservatory, in large pots or growing bags, and move them outdoors as soon as it's reasonably safe to do so. If frost is forecast, bring them in until it's safe to place them outside again. A pot is easy to move, but a growing bag is best placed on a board that two people can easily lift to move in if frost threatens. This sounds a lot of effort when you can pop around to the local shop for them, but a meal or two of freshly harvested young new potatoes really is a treat.

DESIGN TIP *Potatoes are for eating, not admiring, so place the containers where they will not be conspicuous, but make sure they receive plenty of light.*

■ LEFT

OTHER VEGETABLES Marrows, courgettes (zucchini) and cucumbers can all be grown successfully in growing bags or large containers such as half-barrels. This courgette (zucchini) in a half-barrel is beginning to crop.

DESIGN TIP *Marrows and courgettes (zucchini) are decorative, with large yellow flowers. Some varieties have yellow fruit.*

■ BELOW

CONTAINER VEGETABLES If you don't mind giving over a substantial part of your patio to vegetables you can pack in many different kinds. Use large containers that hold plenty of potting soil, and don't neglect the watering.

DESIGN TIP *Large tubs like this are not particularly attractive. You could try decorating them with acrylic paints, or building a low screen tall enough to hide the containers.*

■ RIGHT

USING GROWING BAGS It's surprising what you can raise in a few growing bags. These two contain early potatoes, spinach, lettuce, and salad onions. Choose small varieties or those that can be harvested early.

DESIGN TIP *It may be better to concentrate all your vegetables in one part of the patio, especially if they are in growing bags, otherwise they may begin to detract from the ornamentals.*

Know-how

FRUIT IN FOCUS

Orchards are attractive features in their own right, but they demand considerable space. In small gardens, fruit such as apples, pears and peaches are best grown as cordons, espaliers or fans. These are plants grafted on to a dwarfing rootstock and trained to crop on heavily pruned shoots. Cordons usually have one main stem trained at an angle of about 45°, espaliers have a central upright stem with horizontal tiered branches, and fans have their shoots trained fan-like against a wall or fence. Apples can also be grown in large pots, and some modern varieties have narrow pole-like growth that makes them suitable for a confined space, so they are suitable for even a tiny garden.

■ RIGHT
FLAGPOLE APPLES "Flagpole" apples, of which there are several good varieties available, grow naturally on an upright stem with no branches, but plenty of fruiting spurs. These are ideal trees for a confined space, and you can have a whole collection of them in a small garden.
DESIGN TIP *Try planting a row of different varieties along one boundary of the kitchen garden. They will form a productive screen and boundary marker.*

■ LEFT
STEP-OVER APPLES "Step-over" apples are single espaliers that make a neat edging. They are pretty in flower and attractive in fruit, while taking up the minimum of space. Like all espaliers, they will require annual pruning to maintain their trained shape.
DESIGN TIP *These make a neat and productive edging for a kitchen garden, and would even look attractive at the edge of a flower border.*

■ LEFT
POTTED PEACHES Peaches make attractive fan-trained fruits for a warm position, but this one, known as 'Garden Silver', is growing in bush form in a 30cm (1ft) patio pot. Not all peaches will perform like this in a small pot, however.
DESIGN TIP *Peaches make good patio plants as they are highly ornamental in spring when covered with pink blossom.*

■ ABOVE
CONTAINER APPLES Apples can be grown in large pots, provided they have been grafted on to a very dwarfing rootstock. The crop will be limited but acceptable, and a pot-grown apple always makes a good talking point.
DESIGN TIP *Don't grow apples in containers where you have the choice of planting in the ground – those in the ground don't demand frequent care such as watering. Container-grown apples are best used in paved gardens or on balconies where the options are limited.*

■ ABOVE RIGHT
ESPALIER PEARS This is what is called a productive fence. The espalier 'Conference' pear is laden with fruit and looks highly decorative too.
DESIGN TIP *Try training espalier fruit trees along fences bounding your kitchen garden. They'll look good and release valuable space within the vegetable and fruit bed for planting other fruits.*

■ RIGHT
FAN PEACHES The most decorative way to grow peaches and nectarines, if you want a heavy crop on an ornamental plant, is to grow them as a fan trained against a wall or fence.
DESIGN TIP *Grow a peach against a warm, sunny wall, but don't expect a heavy crop if you live in a cold area.*

Know-how

HERBS

Many herbs are highly ornamental, with pretty flowers and sweet scents, and do not look amiss in flower borders, but herb gardens and herb features make pleasing designs that many people try to incorporate even when the herbs have little culinary attraction.

■ ABOVE
PATIO HERBS Herbs are most likely to be used when planted conveniently for the kitchen rather than tucked away at the end of the garden. The herbs shown are growing in a bed next to the patio, and when you sit on the built-in seat and brush against them, the aromas of the herbs are released.

DESIGN TIP *Place the most ornamental herbs, such as the coloured and variegated sages and chives, towards the front of the bed, with the less attractive kinds such as tarragon and lovage behind. Herb beds can look uninspiring in winter, so try to create a positive setting for them. The garden will then remain attractive long after most of the herbs have died back.*

■ ABOVE

CONTAINER HERBS If space is really tight, a small collection of herbs can be grown in a container like the one shown. Herbs can also be grown in window boxes, but it's probably best to use such valuable space for flowers.

DESIGN TIP *Plant your herbs in an impressive container if it's to be placed in a prominent position. This imitation lead container is made from glass fibre.*

■ ABOVE

HERB BEDS Instead of growing your herbs in rectangular beds, try growing them in beds that form a geometrical pattern. Even when the herbs have died back, this part of the garden will remain interesting due to its strong design.

DESIGN TIP *Give the beds a definite edge to help pick out the shapes and patterns. Here, granite setts have been used to edge the beds and form a contrast with the gravel paths.*

■ ABOVE

HERB WHEEL No matter how small your garden is, it should always be possible to introduce a herb feature. The herb wheel is an old design, especially popular during the nineteenth century. The centrepoint of this design is a variation on the traditional herb wheel.

DESIGN TIP *Introduce this kind of very formal and symmetrical feature only if you have the time to spend keeping the herbs trimmed. While the shape remains well defined, a herb wheel makes an excellent focal point, but if the plants are allowed to become overgrown and mask the outline of the rim and spokes, much of the effect is lost.*

Know-how

AN INTEGRATED APPROACH

If you can't bring yourself to devote part of your garden to vegetables and herbs alone, consider integrating as many as possible with the ornamentals. Many are quite pretty in their own right, and when merged with other ornamentals they can work surprisingly well.

■ LEFT
POTAGER In a potager, flowers and vegetables are grown together without strict demarcation lines. You will probably either love this effect or find it disconcerting – it's not the kind of feature many find visually neutral.
DESIGN TIP *A potager is best given its own area of the garden, perhaps separated from the purely ornamental part of the garden by a dwarf hedge or perhaps a picket fence.*

■ RIGHT
FORMAL VEGETABLE GARDEN Try creating a formal garden with beds edged by dwarf box (*Buxus sempervirens* 'Suffruticosa'), and planting ornamental plants in some and vegetables in others. It will make an unusual and surprisingly interesting garden.
DESIGN TIP *Plant the beds that had vegetables in summer with winter-flowering bulbs and spring bedding. That way you'll gain more ornamental value without sacrificing much in terms of crops.*

■ ABOVE

ORNAMENTAL VEGETABLES
Rhubarb chard is a spectacular plant
whether grown in rows in the vegetable
garden, or used with summer bedding
plants. Here it has been used as a
centrepiece of the bed with lobelia
around the edge.
DESIGN TIP *Rhubarb chard makes a
pleasing "dot" plant to bring height to
summer bedding schemes. Even if you
don't like the taste and have no desire to
harvest it, consider using this plant as an
arresting ornamental foliage plant.*

■ ABOVE

MIXED GARDENS In this cottage
garden blue cornflowers (*Centaurea
cyanus*) rub shoulders with blue borage,
while all around is a wide range of
vegetables. Anyone who likes a neat
and tidy garden with plants in distinct
"compartments" will find this kind of
garden disturbing, but it has a special
charm and has the benefit of deterring

pests and diseases because of the
diversity of plants grown.
DESIGN TIP *If the rest of the garden is
formal in style, separate this kind of
feature with a hedge or screen, otherwise
the apparent chaos of this style of vegetable
growing will be emphasized. It doesn't
matter in a cottage garden, where plants
often merge into one another.*

■ RIGHT

PLANTING FOR HARVESTING
Beetroot has beautiful foliage that we
often take for granted. Here it is being
grown as an ornamental, but you could
clear it to harvest then replant the
vacated space with something else.
DESIGN TIP *If you want to harvest a
crop, it's best to plant in separate blocks
where the space can easily be replanted,
rather than interplanting with flowers,
which can make harvesting difficult and
leave unattractive gaps afterwards.*

Planning and Planting

KITCHEN CORNER

Where there's space, it's a good idea to position the kitchen garden to one side of the house, perhaps partitioned by a hedge. Here a warm corner has been put to good use as an attractive herb garden.

PLANNING

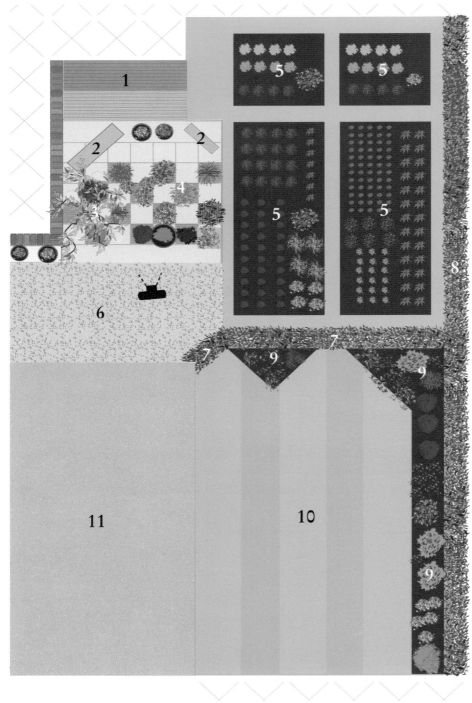

HERB WHEELS

Herb wheels are charming and popular features that display herbs to their best advantage. They are sometimes made out of old cart or wagon wheels, but these are not easy to obtain. It's far easier to adapt the concept and make a brick "wheel". The larger the "wheel" the more "spokes" you can introduce.

Allocate a contrasting colour, scent or leaf shape to each bed within the spokes to give definition to the wheel.

MAKING A HERB WHEEL

1 Mark a circle about 1.5–1.8m (5–6ft) across, using a line fixed to a peg to ensure an even shape. If it helps, use a wine bottle filled with dry sand instead of a stick to mark out the perimeter. Excavate the ground to a depth of about 15cm (6in).

PLANTING

2 Place bricks on end, or at an angle, around the edge. If you place them at a 45° angle it will create a dog-tooth effect; bricks placed on end will look more formal. Either lay them loose in compacted earth, or bed them on mortar.

3 Lay rows of brick, cross-fashion, as shown. If the diameter does not allow for them to be laid without gaps in the centre, stand an ornament or pot in the middle if you are not planting directly into the soil in that position.

4 Top up the areas between the "spokes" with good garden or potting soil. Add fertilizer at this point, if necessary.

5 Plant up each section, using plants that will balance each other in size of growth if possible. You could, for instance, grow a collection of different thymes. For a smart finish, carefully cover the soil with fine gravel.

Planning and Planting

ORNAMENTAL KITCHEN GARDEN

The vegetables don't have to be tucked away out of sight. You can mix them with flowers, and enclose both in formal dwarf box hedges to create a wonderful ornamental kitchen garden with lots of style.

This plan shows a kitchen garden laid out in formal style, where there is space to make a long-term feature of it. Although box hedges grow reasonably rapidly, it will take perhaps four or five years to form neatly clipped hedges like those

shown in the photograph.

Growing vegetables in an ornamental setting like this, and being prepared to plant and sow flowers among them, makes a kitchen garden to be admired and not just used.

PLANNING

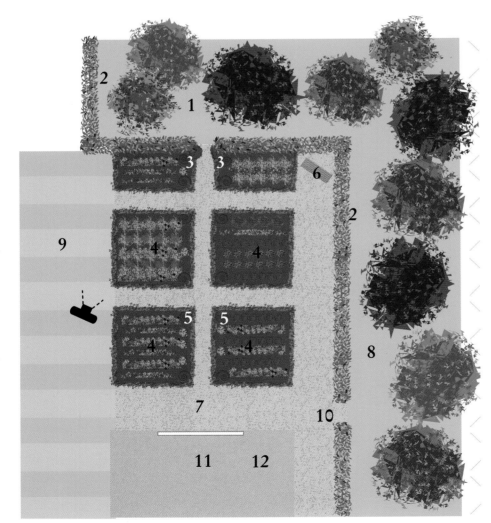

PRUNING CORDON AND ESPALIER APPLES

Cordons and espaliers are frequently used in small gardens because they are more decorative than bush forms, and they save space. The drawback is that they require regular pruning – once in summer and again in winter on old plants that have become congested. This winter pruning is only to thin out the number of spurs (short, stubby shoots) when they have become so congested that there is insufficient space for the fruits to develop properly.

A single-tiered espalier – sometimes called step-over training – can be used for a fruitful edging to the beds instead of, say, a dwarf box edging.

PLANTING

HOW TO PRUNE ESPALIERS

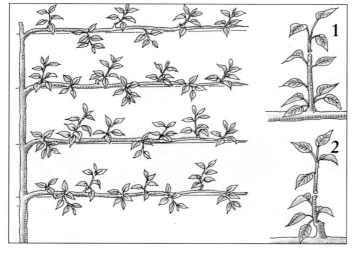

1 Shorten new leafy shoots that have grown directly from the main branches back to three leaves above the basal cluster of leaves. This should only be done once the shoots have dark green leaves and the bark has started to turn brown and is woody at the base. In cold areas it may be early autumn before the shoots are mature enough.

2 If the shoot is growing from a stub left by previous pruning – and not directly from one of the main stems – cut back to one leaf above the basal cluster of leaves.

HOW TO PRUNE CORDONS

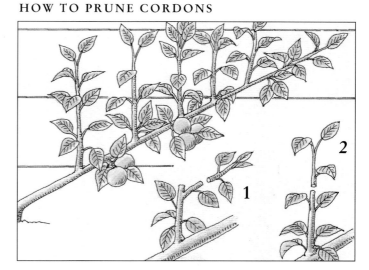

1 Cut back shoots growing from stubs left by earlier pruning to one leaf above the basal cluster.

2 A cordon is pruned in the same way as an espalier, though the basic shape of the plant is different. Cut back shoots growing directly from the main branch to three leaves above the basal cluster of leaves.

Planning and Planting

PIVOTING ON CIRCLES

This plan shows what can be achieved in a relatively small garden only 11m x 9m (36ft x 30ft), and should be an inspiration for all who think that you need a large garden to come up with an imaginative design that's packed with innovative features.

PLANNING

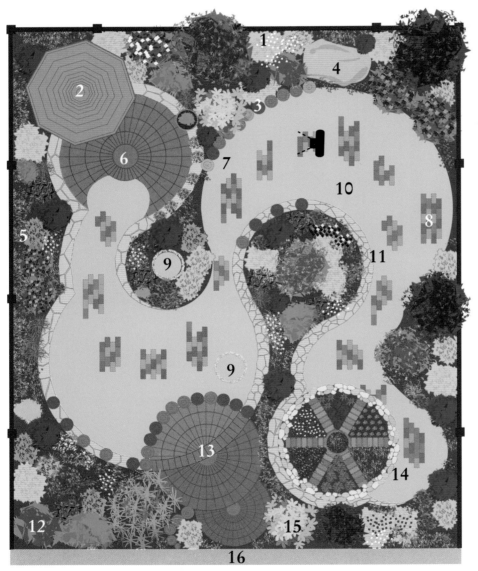

The number of herbs you can grow in even a large herb wheel is limited, and tall ones such as fennel are unsuitable. To accommodate the larger types and increase the range of herbs available, the border closest to the house and herb wheel has also been planted with various aromatic herbs. By including plenty of shrubby ones, such as coloured and variegated sages, this kind of border can look highly attractive and scent the air near the house.

PATIO HERB FEATURES

If your patio is looking drab and in need of colour, lift a few of the paving slabs to plant patches of brightly coloured or scented herbs. Try to remove the slabs without breaking them, and save them for another purpose. Remember that many herbs will look effective for only part of the year, so choose your plants carefully.

As this plan shows, herbs can be worked into a highly ornamental garden without sacrificing anything in terms of beauty or impact. This garden was initially designed with a shallow circular pool where the herb wheel is positioned now, but to demonstrate how easy it is to modify an existing plan to suit a particular need, we've made this area into an attractive herb garden.

PLANTING

HOW TO PLANT A PATIO HERB FEATURE

1 Lift the paving slabs using a cold chisel and club hammer. They will come up fairly easily if bedded on sand or blobs of mortar, but if laid over a concrete base it will be necessary to break up the concrete. In which case it may be preferable to build a small raised bed for your herbs instead.

2 The ground will have become compacted and may be composed of impoverished sub soil. Start by breaking it up with a fork, then add a generous amount of planting mixture or rotted garden compost. Dig it in thoroughly.

3 It is important to give the feature some height, so plant a large herb in the centre. This is a bay (*Laurus nobilis*), but you could use rosemary (*Rosmarinus officinalis*).

4 Plant up with herbs of your choice. Here golden marjorams are being planted in one corner.

Planning and Planting

FOCUS ON HERBS

A geometric herb garden makes a super feature whether or not you have a culinary need, and is often planted with medicinal and cosmetic herbs purely for their decorative and historic interest. A feature like this is sometimes more decorative than useful, in which case the emphasis should be on aesthetically pleasing planting rather than only herbs that you hope to harvest.

PLANNING

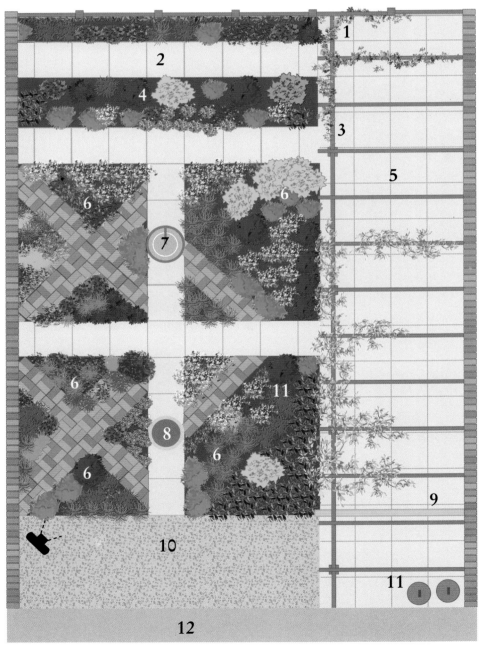

Herb gardens are popular features, but they require structure and year-round focal points such as a sundial or birdbath to retain interest, when they have died back for winter. In a formal herb garden like this, paths play an important role – they mark out the beds but also form the main structural element during the winter months. It is important that these are attractive and well laid. Brick is a popular choice, but clay pavers are a good alternative. To break up the ground textures, paving slabs have also been used in this design.

WHAT TYPE OF SOIL?

Whether planting ornamentals or edibles, it's a good idea to test your soil. It will tell you which plants will thrive, and whether to improve your soil to grow particular plants.

Some kits test only for pH (which tells you how acid or alkaline your soil is). The test opposite is for nitrogen, but the same instructions will apply to most other kits.

PLANTING

HOW TO TEST YOUR SOIL

1 Collect a soil sample from about 5–8cm (2–3in) below the surface. Take a number of samples from around the garden and either test each of them separately or mix them in one test.

2 With this kit one part of soil is mixed with five parts of water. Shake vigorously in a clean jar, then allow the soil particles to settle – this could take half an hour to a day, depending on the soil.

3 Using the pipette provided in the kit, draw off some of the liquid from the top few centimetres (about an inch) when the mixture has settled.

4 Transfer the solution to the test and reference chambers in the plastic container, using the pipette.

5 Select the appropriate test capsule, and empty the powder into the test chamber. Replace the cap, then shake vigorously.

6 After a few minutes, compare the colour of the liquid with the shade panel that forms part of the container. The kit will explain the meaning of each reading, and what – if anything – needs to be done.

Planning and Planting

FORMAL BUT DECORATIVE

Celebrate the tasty delights of the kitchen garden with a formal but decorative design that makes even the humble cabbage look ornamental, and provides space for cut flowers, too. This style of kitchen garden may be less practical than a rectangular plot where the crops are grown in long rows, but it's far more decorative.

PLANNING

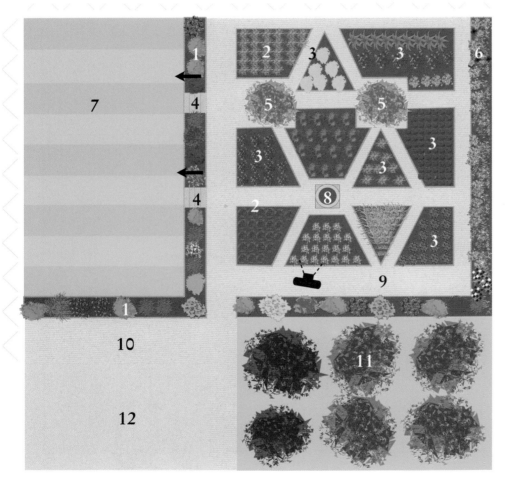

KEY TO PLAN

1 Dwarf shrubs on bank
2 Sweet-pea teepee surrounded by vegetables
3 Vegetables
4 Steps to lower lawn
5 Pear tree
6 Annual cut-flower border
7 Lawn on lower level
8 Urn on plinth
9 Stone and earth path
10 Gravel
11 Orchard
12 House

✕ Garden continues

← Direction of steps down

⚘ Viewpoint on photograph

GROWING VEGETABLES IN SMALL BEDS

There are many advantages to growing vegetables in small beds. You can do all the cultivation without walking on the soil and compacting it, so no-dig systems are a practical option. With these techniques, the only digging to be done is that needed to clear the ground of weeds initially and to incorporate lots of organic material such as rotted manure or garden compost at the same time. Subsequently, more organic material is added to the surface as a mulch, and this is worked into the soil by worms and other creatures. If lots of organic material is added regularly, the soil fertility and structure will be improved each year, and crop yield will certainly benefit.

As this kitchen garden is quite close to the house, a formal design with a patchwork of small beds has been chosen to make a decorative contribution to the garden as well as a culinary one.

Starting with clear ground it would have been possible to devise a more traditional and strictly symmetrical design, but the presence of a couple of old pear trees dictated a more flexible approach. Although the beds do not create a symmetrical design, there is the suggestion of a regular pattern, and the idiosyncratic shapes add to the charm of this interesting kitchen garden.

PLANTING

■ **ABOVE**
These beds are of irregular size because they form part of a larger pattern of beds, but even the larger ones are not difficult to cultivate from the surrounding pathways.

■ **ABOVE**
A traditional vegetable plot can be converted into a 1.2m (4ft) bed system simply by sowing in short rows and doing all the cultivation from the paths between them.

Some gardeners using this system use only organic manures and fertilizers and achieve wonderful crops without manufactured fertilizers. Small beds help because the lack of soil compaction means the soil structure is not harmed, and it's easier for worms and insects to work the manures and composts into the soil.

No-dig systems can be achieved on a traditional vegetable plot by dividing the area into 1.2m (4ft) strips, which makes cultivation from the paths practical without standing on the soil.

■ **LEFT**
A potager is an area where vegetables and flowers are grown together. The flowers are often cut for floral decoration, and in this garden each bed has a teepee of sweet peas to provide a supply of cut flowers for the home.

Planning and Planting
CREATING A HERB GARDEN

Herbs are the most attractive of all plants grown in the kitchen garden, and for that reason decorative herb gardens are popular features. In a large garden, it's worth setting aside a separate, enclosed area in which a herb garden like this can be created. It will be a place in which to sit and relax, and if you plant whole beds of one kind of herb, you'll be able to harvest plenty without spoiling the decorative effect.

PLANNING

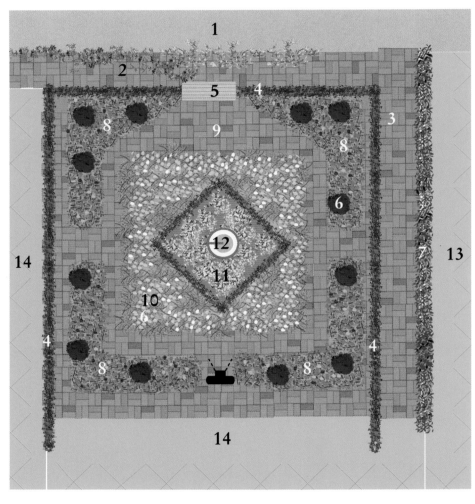

KEY TO PLAN

1 Garage
2 Climbers against garage wall
3 Path
4 Dwarf box (*Buxus sempervirens* 'Suffruticosa') hedge
5 Garden bench
6 Clipped box (*Buxus sempervirens*)
7 Yew hedge
8 Thyme
9 Brick paving
10 Chives
11 Golden marjoram
12 Sundial
13 To orchard
14 To house
✕ Garden continues
⬛ Viewpoint on photograph

A herb garden like this will make a culinary contribution, but it should really be viewed primarily as a decorative feature. Instead of growing a few plants of many different kinds of herbs, which might be more practical for kitchen use, making a bold splash with a few of the most decorative herbs creates a more striking visual feature and imparts a stronger sense of design.

Herb gardens like this depend on a symmetrical design, but they require a strong centrepiece around which the garden hangs – here an attractive sundial. An edging of box helps to hold the design together when it forms part of a larger garden.

GROWING HERBS IN CONTAINERS
Even if you have a large herb garden like the one shown in the plan and photograph here, a small container packed with a collection of herbs would be useful close to the kitchen door.

If you simply don't have space for a proper herb garden, a feature like the wine-case herb box shown opposite, will provide the occasional picking of fresh leaves and it looks good too.

PLANTING

HOW TO MAKE A WINE-CASE HERB FEATURE

1 Remove any wire staples from around the edges of an old wine case, and sand down rough edges. Apply two coats of exterior varnish, inside and out. Allow the varnish to dry thoroughly between coats.

2 Place broken pots or similar drainage material in the bottom of the box, then stand the pots of herbs in the container to work out the best arrangement.

3 Fill the box with a gritty potting soil, then start planting. Loosen a few of the roots from the rootball before planting to encourage the plant to root. Finish planting, then sprinkle a slow-release fertilizer over the surface. Water well, then cover the surface with a mulch such as finely chipped bark.

4 Stand the finished container within ready reach of the kitchen, and remember to keep it well watered. Harvest only a small amount of leaves each time if you want it to remain an ornamental feature.

Choosing Plants
PLANTS FOR KITCHEN GARDENS

When it comes to edible crops, you'll grow what you like and not what necessarily gives the heaviest crops or looks the most pleasing. Flavour is everything when growing for your own consumption. Our suggestions here are for crops that are likely to give a good yield for the space and effort, or that are interesting and deserve to be better known. In the case of herbs, our suggestions are for those that are decorative as well as of culinary merit – if space for a kitchen garden is limited, you can grow these in flower and shrub borders, or in window boxes, containers, planting spaces on patios or between paving slabs.

EASY SALADS
A collection of salad crops must surely include lettuce or endive, and of course tomatoes. If you consider these uninteresting, try red lettuce and perhaps yellow tomatoes. Sow lettuces little and often for succession. Tomatoes crop best under glass in cooler climates, but they are less trouble to look after outdoors, especially if you choose a bush type that does not require the removal of sideshoots. Radishes are ready within weeks when growing

Lettuce 'Lolla Rossa' forms a loose ball-shaped head, but you can pick individual leaves if you don't need the whole head at once. The crisp and tangy, frilly leaves add a touch of colour to a summer salad.

conditions are good, but they'll disappoint if not sown little and often as they deteriorate rapidly if not harvested regularly.

For out-of-season salads, consider some of the less common leafy vegetables such as corn salad.

Endive makes a refreshing change from lettuce, but it tastes better if blanched for a few days before harvesting. Unlike lettuce, it will also tolerate a few degrees of frost. This variety is 'Green Curled'.

UNUSUAL OR INTERESTING VEGETABLES
Growing ordinary vegetables may become inspiring, and most of them you can buy readily in your local supermarket. Growing your own provides an opportunity to experiment with some of the more

Rhubarb chard is one of the few vegetables that most of us would be happy to include in the flower garden. Sometimes it is even used in summer bedding displays.

This strange-looking and decorative vegetable is called a custard marrow or patty pan squash.

interesting kinds, or varieties that may not be profitable commercial crops but have a good flavour, such as the 'Pink Fir Apple' potato, with its knobbly tubers. Asparagus peas are quite decorative with their red flowers and angular seed pods, while Swiss chard and rhubarb chard are leafy plants that are highly ornamental. Instead of the ordinary marrow (squash), try the custard marrow (patty pan squash) with its distinctive flattish fruits with scalloped edges.

DECORATIVE HERBS

Many herbs can be grown as ornamentals in the shrub border: rosemary, sage, and bay, for example. Others, such as marjorams, chives, golden lemon balm and borage, are ideal for a

Chives are deservedly one of the most widely grown herbs. Their grass-like leaves and pretty pink flowers in summer make them very ornamental, and they are sometimes planted as an edging.

mixed or herbaceous border. Thymes are happy in a rock garden. All of those mentioned, with the exception of borage, also make pleasing container plants.

PICK OF THE FRUITS

Tree fruits are particularly rewarding to grow, as the crop is often heavy for a given area, and the cropping lasts for many weeks, usually months if fruits such as apples and pears are stored. Apples and pears can also be bought trained as fans, cordons and espaliers, which are ideal for a small garden.

If growing soft fruit, make sure you grow for flavour to make the effort worthwhile (and be sure to protect them from birds). You can buy huge and luscious-looking

strawberries in shops or markets, but some of the varieties with smaller fruits may have a better, often sweeter, flavour.

'Waltz', one of the apple varieties that grows like a pole without normal side branches, the fruit being produced on spurs close to the main stem. These are ideal for a tiny garden where you also require a vertical tree.

Pears don't have to be grown as large trees. This 'Beurre Hardy' is growing as a decorative fan, and picking is easy.

Sage is a compact shrub that looks good towards the front of a shrub border. *Salvia officinalis* itself is green, but there are varieties with attractive variegation in gold or shades of pink and purple, which are often grown as ornamentals.

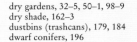

INDEX

ACKNOWLEDGEMENTS

The author and publisher are grateful to acknowledge the work of Robert Crawford Clarke, who has extrapolated the plans for the gardens. These plans do not necessarily reflect the original designer's plan. Where known, the existing garden designers are acknowledged below.

t = top, b = bottom, l = left, r = right, m = middle

Front cover: (Godfrey Amy's Garden, Jersey, Anthony Paul Design)
A–Z Botanical Collection Ltd: p65tr Sylvia O'Toole; p75tl Mike Vardy; p145t; p174 James Braidwood; p175t Adrian Thomas (design by Wendy Bundy); p229t A. Stenning; p241t Adrian Thomas.
Pat Brindley: p3; p34t; p51t; p117b; p175b.
Jonathan Buckley: p2; p4; p81t; p114; p29b; p142; p170; p213; p226.
The Garden Picture Library: p1 (designer Clay Perry); p5 Steven Wooster (John Brookes Design); p7 Gil Hanly (Nan Raymond Garden, New Zealand); p8 Gil Hanly (Ethidge Gardens, Timaru, Canterbury, New Zealand, Nan and Wynne Raymond; p19 Gil Hanly (Penny Zino Garden, Flaxmere, Hawarden, New Zealand); p30 Henk Dijkman; p32 J. S. Sira; p33t Ron Sutherland (Michelle Osborne Design); p33b Ron Sutherland (Smyth Garden, Jersey, Anthony Paul Design); p34b Ron Sutherland (Paul Bangay Design); p35t Ron Sutherland (Chelsea Flower Show, London, Hiroshi Nanamori Design); p35b Jerry Pavia;); p39m David Askham; p39bl Steven Wooster (Sticky Wicket, Dorset; p45 Ron Sutherland (Murray Collis Design, Australia); p47t J. S. Sira; p49t, l Ron Sutherland (Paul Bangay Design); p55l Ron Sutherland (Anthony Paul Design); p58 J. S. Sira (Chelsea Flower Show, London); p59 Brigitte Thomas; p60t Jerry Pavia; p60b Ron Sutherland; p61 Henk Dijkman; p62 Steven Wooster; p63t Marijke Heuff; p63b Ron Sutherland (John Zerning Balcony); p64bl Friedrich Strauss; p68b Ron Sutherland (Anthony Paul Design); p73tl Ron Sutherland (Eco Design, Melbourne, Australia); p77t Ron Sutherland (Anthony Paul Design); p79t Brigitte Thomas; p86 J. S. Sira (design by Japanse Garden Company, Chelsea Flower Show, London 1991); p88 Ron Sutherland (Paul Flinton Design, Australia); p89t Lamontagne; p89b Alan Mitchell; p90 Ron Sutherland (Anthony Paul Design); p91b Ron Sutherland (Anthony Paul Design); p96b Ron Sutherland (Paul Flemming Design, Australia); p101t Lamontagne; p103t Ron Sutherland; p105l Ron Sutherland (Paul Flemming Design, Australia); p107t Ron Sutherland (Hiroshi Nanamori Design); p109b Ron Sutherland (Anthony Paul

Design); p115 Brigitte Thomas (Preen Manor, Shropshire; p116 Ron Sutherland (Anthony Paul Design); p117t John Glover; p118 Ron Sutherland; p119t Ron Sutherland (Anthony Paul Design); p119b Steven Wooster (Duane Paul Design Team, Chelsea Flower Show); p131 Jerry Pavia; p135 Brian Carter (Van Hage Design); p139 Steven Wooster (Mailstone Landscaping); p147b John Neubauer (Solomon Garden, Washington); p152b Steven Wooster (Julie Toll Design, John Chamber's Garden, Chelsea Flower Show, 1990); p153t Mayer/Le Scanff (Jardin de Campagne, France); p163t Steven Wooster (Gordon Collet Design); p172b Ron Sutherland (Paul Flemming Design, Melbourne, Australia); p173 Gil Hanley(Bruce Cornish Garden, Auckland); p187bl John Glover; p195t Marianne Majerus (John Brooks Design, BBC Garden); p198 J. S. Sira (Action for Blind People, Chelsea Flower Show, 1991); p200 Steven Wooster (designer H. Weijers); p201t Marie O'Hara; p203 Brian Carter (design by Geoff and Faith Whitten, Chelsea Flower Show, London 1989); p217 Ron Sutherland (Michael Balston Design); p219b Ron Sutherland (Rick Eckersley Design); p221 Ron Sutherland (Godfrey Amy's Garden, Jersey, Anthony Paul Design); p223t David Askham.
Robert Harding Picture Library: p66t Ian Baldwin Pool; p189t James Merrell; p191b BBC Enterprises/Redwood Publishing (design by David Sanford); p193t BBC Enterprises/Redwood Publishing (design by Jean Bishop).
Houses & Interiors: p165t; p201b.
Andrew Lawson Photographic: p171.
Peter McHoy: p9 (David Sanford); p23; p25; p31; p36; p37; p38; p39t; p40; p41; p42; p43; p51bl, br; p 53 (design by Kathleen McHoy) p53b; p56; p57; p65tr, bl; p66; p67; p68t; p69b; p.70; p71; p83t; p84tr; p84br; p85; p87; p92; p93; p94; p95; p96t; p.97; p98; p99; p107b; p111; p112; p113l, mb, r; p120; p121; p122; p123; p124; p125; p126; p126b (design by Alpine Garden Society); p127; p133 (design by Natural and Oriental Water Gardens); p137; p140m, bl; p141m; p141tr; p145b; p146; p147t; p148; p149; p150; p151; p153b; p154t; p155b; p157t; p159t; p161b (design by Jean Bishop); p167t; p168; p169; p172t; p176b; p177b; p178; p179; p180l; p181b; p183l, bl; p196t, c, b; p197; p199; p202; p205; p206t b; p207t, b; p208t,b; p209b; p215t; p219tl. tr; p224t, br, bl; p225; p227; p228; p229b; p230; p231t, b; p232t, b; p233t,c, b; p234t, b; p235; p236; p237; p238t,b; p239; p243t; p245 (design by Christopher Costin); p245; p249tr, c, b; p252; p253; p254; p255; p256.
Harry Smith Horticultural Collection: p26; p143; p144.
Derek St Romaine: p249l; p251t.